ASPARAGUS DREAMS

of related interest

Pretending to be Normal
Living with Asperger's Syndrome
Liane Holliday Willey
ISBN 978 1 85302 749 9

Making Sense of the Unfeasible
My Life Journey with Asperger Syndrome
Marc Fleisher
ISBN 978 1 84310 165 9

Asperger's Syndrome
A Guide for Parents and Professionals
Tony Attwood
ISBN 978 1 85302 577 8

Asperger Syndrome in Adolescence
Living with the Ups, the Downs and Things in Between
Edited by Liane Holliday Willey
ISBN 978 1 84310 742 2

Freaks, Geeks and Asperger Syndrome
A User Guide to Adolescence
Luke Jackson
ISBN 978 1 84310 098 0

Haze
An Asperger Novel
Kathy Hoopmann
ISBN 978 1 84310 072 0

ASPARAGUS DREAMS

Jessica Peers

Jessica Kingsley Publishers
London and Philadelphia

First published in the United Kingdom in 2003
by Jessica Kingsley Publishers
116 Pentonville Road
London N1 9JB, UK
and
400 Market Street, Suite 400
Philadelphia, PA 19106, USA

www.jkp.com

Library of Congress Cataloging in Publication Data
A CIP catalog record for this book is available from the Library of Congress

British Library Cataloguing in Publication Data
A CIP catalogue record for this book is available from the British Library

ISBN 978 1 84310 164 2

For Les Peers
1948–2001

CONTENTS

– INTRODUCTION –

Like a cat hiding behind the bushes, my Asperger's syndrome is sometimes difficult to spot. However, like a cat, this side of me catches the little things in life: the small details that people usually ignore. Trapped and collected, the images are here. Told with an aspy's-eye viewpoint, here is my tale.

Diagnosed at the age of twelve, I was expelled from mainstream education. Believing myself to be "normal", despite the obvious quirks of my behaviour, I was sent to a school for adolescents affected by varying degrees on the autistic spectrum. My stay here spanned from 1990 to 1995 and is documented in this book.

This book is not accusatory or dictatorial. Although some residents were misunderstood (including myself) and suffered great unhappiness at their misguided treatment, I have not launched a thinly veiled attack, as this, I feel, would be pointless. Time has moved on, and people have moved on; this is understood.

Many of the characters are composite, and names have been altered to save embarrassment to those concerned. Some of these characters I still meet, and they remain my friends.

I have decided to share my experiences so a more enlightened view towards both Asperger's and autism may be encouraged.

– ONE –

MY MOTHER DROVE a battered old Vauxhall Chevette. Due to an incident concerning a long-preserved chocolate stain behind the back window, it had been nicknamed the Star Bar Car. Disfigured by a fresh black wing-replacement, jarring loudly against its plump yellow body, many had likened it to some sort of demented bee. I thought of it more as a large mechanical frog, complete with sweaty hatchback and vinyl roof. The floor, littered with empty crisp packets and sweet wrappers, was stained grey with cigarette ash.

Sat in the back, behind my mother and father, I sighed with relief that my sisters were not with me. They would only be playing stupid car-games and making in-jokes with each other. These jokes I could never understand. I was always the outsider to their singing, laughing inside. Usually the jokes were at my expense. I was glad to be alone on the back seat. I had brought pop music magazines along to keep me occupied. Pop music never called me names or giggled behind my back, never told me off for eating too many sweets or sleeping in until two o'clock in the afternoon.

Summer had died slowly, leaving behind only the ringing of an overplayed radio. The days and nights had merged into one, rather like Play-Doh, once colourful now blended into a sludgy grey-brown, stretched out into a long, tapering roll. Expelled from school, I had sat on the floor of my room, burning holes in the carpet with my knees as I doodled on pieces of white paper. The door had remained locked as I had created characters in my own world. Sometimes I had felt like an invisible God, creating a cartoon universe on that paper. Nobody saw it. If they did, that part of my universe would be ripped up and thrown in the bin.

The hot sun would burn down outside as my sisters played with the kids across the road. I would hide away, fearing taunts. In my bedroom I was safe. The radio would play as I listed chart-numbers of songs on my paper. With my supply of crisps and chocolate by my side, I would enjoy the freedom of my voluntary imprisonment. My loneliness was purposeful. I was safe.

Dad said I looked pale and was putting on weight. I still ate and stayed in. I had no friends to meet, no places to go to. I would read books from Mum's library, sometimes two in one day. The characters in books were my friends, just like the radio and sweets. Safe.

I was leaving my safety. Half afraid, half excited, I studied my hair in the wing-mirror over Dad's shoulder. Once long, it was now mutilated into that eternally unflattering style known as a *bob*. With a thick, greasy fringe that obscured my eyes, the ends flicked out rather than curled under. I could see a spot forming on my chin. *Ugly*. I was not pretty, like Kylie Minogue or Madonna. How I wished I could look like a pop star or model. This was another reason why I hid away. I was often teased for being a mess, for being scruffy. Even if I tidied myself up, I was still *ugly*.

Walking up the smooth concrete of the pathway to Easton House, through a freshly trimmed arbour of pink roses, I felt my pink suede flat shoes trudge nervously against the ground. The knees of my baggy jeans were crusted with carpet-muck and Blu-Tack. Before me, I saw the doorbell. Against it, I bravely placed my finger.

"This is a place," said Mum proudly, with the air of a stage actress, "where there is no bullying." Placing her cigarettes back inside her huge leather handbag, she added with enforced jollity, "There are no bullies, no gangs, just people your own age with similar difficulties. You'll make lots of new friends."

I was hugged and kissed as I read the sign above the letterbox: "Something…Something AUTISTIC Society."

Surely they had spelt "artistic" wrong. Mum had always told me I was "artistic". I knew I had Asparagus syndrome. That had been mentioned before. I was also very good at art, or so people would always say. Maybe the word "Autistic" was a creative mistake. I sure as Hell didn't know what it meant.

At this point I began to worry. What if I had been sent to the wrong place? What if the word was not a mistake? What if it had a meaning I did not know?

Shrugging, I filled my head with illusions: this was a school for young, *gifted* people, creative people like myself. Teenagers of all shapes, sizes and colours would welcome me into their little circles. We would sit around painting, sculpting, writing and making music. At night, we would stay up late watching horror films, then laugh and joke, telling wild tales to one another as friends.

My thirteen-and-a-bit years of impetuousness recoiled within my blue-brown jeans as the door opened.

"Hello. You must be Jennifer," smiled an abnormally tall woman with even taller hair.

"*Jessica!*" I corrected her beneath my breath.

"Enjoy your stay," smiled Mum, hugging and kissing me again. Both parents waved from the car.

"Do well, kid," said Dad as the car drove away.

I was alone with these strangers who greeted me, but I remembered coping well at the clinic. It was at the clinic that I had been diagnosed with Asparagus syndrome. That probably just meant that I was a bit rebellious and prone to mood-swings and making my animal-noises. It was probably just another invented "mental" problem, like the ones people at school had told me I possessed.

I had been the stranger at school. Others had said I was taken over by demons and had thrown chewing-gum in my hair. They had called me a psycho because I said and did *strange things*. Me, being me, I had thought that they were the strange ones. Once, I had been stood on the step of the prefab, like a circus attraction, after throwing a ruler at mad Miss Defty, the maths teacher. She had deserved it, I thought, for ignoring me again in class.

Mental, people had said I was *mental*. The word no longer hurt. It was my surname now: Jessica Mental. It had a hollow ring. I wasn't like other girls, couldn't understand boys. Boys just said I was ugly and weird. They would ask me out on dates only so they could laugh in my face with a gang of their allies.

I hated P.E. Always a deep-fielder at rounders, I was never good enough to bowl or stand on a base. In truth, I was purposely lazy, always trying to avoid the crowd. Teamwork was not my strength. However, I was good at cross-country and long-distance running. Blinkered, I would just run straight ahead, striding away from the gangs who trudged along behind me. They would smoke and gossip, rather than run. I would continue towards the finishing-line. I felt free when I ran. As my feet pounded the earth, I would stride away, my mind filled with thoughts. The mad world of Jessica Mental was allowed to flourish.

After sport, I dreaded the showers. After removing the daisy-chains formed from boredom from around my neck, I would splash myself with water in pretence that I had showered. My legs, covered in thick, black hair, remained covered, as did my flat chest. I had once trimmed the hairs with a pair of blunt scissors, as Mum had told me I was too young to shave. Under my vest lay a teetotal beer-belly and a chest flatter than a table. I wanted to strangle the Flake girl on the adverts. She was perfect! However, I knew that she was a chocolate-mime, not a chocolate-eater, like myself.

If anyone ever yelled at me in P.E., or told me I was doing something wrong, or ignored me altogether, I would scream. Then, cleverly, I would fall into a carefully acted swoon. I would play dead, lying perfectly still. Many times I had played comatose. Once, I had faked an entire epileptic fit to drop out of a race. Needless to say, I had always done well in drama class.

Often, people said my behaviour was "melodramatic", that I would fall or cry if I was hit.

When bullies hit, I would hit back, gaining no reward, only the blame for starting the fight. One day I hit back too hard: the action that caused my expulsion.

Rick was a small kid, a year younger than me, but popular for his often cruel and tasteless sense of humour. Knowing that I had a lack of friends and struggled with my weight, he would single me out for his games of "Kick the Fat Mama". Bending over the pool table, I heard him sneak up behind me. Slapping me across the backside, he ran away, laughing. Trying to ignore him, I fetched my schoolbag to do my homework. Suddenly, I felt a slap across my cheek.

"Hey Fat Mama!" he sang, then "Big Girls Don't Cry!".

Turning around, my instincts made me grab the perpetrator. Before I knew it, I was holding him up against the wall. Suddenly and violently, I felt myself smack his head against the plaster. Stunned, he burst into tears.

Staring down at the sobbing heap on the floor, I realised what I had done. Horrified, I began to apologise. I knew that I would be expelled, yet I was glad that Rick had met his comeuppance. Violence usually solved nothing, but I had been uncontrollable, driven to my limits. I had put up with Rick's taunting for too long, a taunting he was never questioned or cautioned about.

My parents were enraged, my mother shouting and howling and threatening me, my father pointing his finger and lecturing me over my crime. Eventually, they had found me a new school, one where they promised there would be no bullying.

"Come in," said the tall woman, breaking my train of thought.

The smile was false, painted onto her pastel-glossed lips, the grey eyes, behind thick glasses, staring above my head towards the road outside. Behind her, I heard a muffled whine as a tiny, crouched, dark-haired girl was frog-marched across the hallway.

"Hi," I smiled innocently, "I'm Jessica. What's your name?"

No reply.

"That's Elena. I wouldn't talk to her right now." The tall woman tilted her head, knowingly.

"Why not?" I asked, before moving on to my favourite question: "How old is she?" The girl looked scarcely twelve years old, far too young to be in a place for adolescents.

"Sixteen."

"*Sixteen?* Eh, God! But she's so…so…" I refrained from saying "*Tiny!*"

Elena was a lot smaller than myself, and drowned in a sea of uncomfortable *cute*-ness. Slight of build, her body, especially the shoulders, seemed strangely twisted. Mediterranean and elfin-looking, her diminutive form lay swamped beneath an enormous, blanket-sized Minnie Mouse sweater. Tearing at her hair with her pincers, she defiantly threw her scrunchie down onto the floor before gnawing at her shoulder. I thought of a rodent caught in a trap.

Swallowing heavily, I could not help but stare. Perhaps she had been called "mental" at school also. Two assistants ran to grab the girl.

"I'm Stacey," said the tall woman, totally unperturbed by the fracas behind her.

"Hi, Stacey," I replied, unsmiling. "What's my first lesson? Are you a teacher? Do you do sport here? Can I miss P.E. and just do drama? Is that allowed? Do I get detention for doing *bad things?*"

I realised that I was asking too many questions, yet my tongue continued to fire them from its cannon. Near breathless, I reached a silence and found myself staring hard into the grey eyes of Stacey.

"Why don't you go sit in the common room and relax for a little bit?" asked Stacey, clearly reciting some kind of premeditated line. She had not heard my questions.

"Was Elena bullied at school?" I continued, still staring her in the eye.

"No. She never went to school."

"So she wasn't expelled?"

"No. She never went to school."

"How come she never went to school? Was she home-taught? Did she have rich parents and a personal tutor? Or did she just not go to school? Like, was she poorly or something?"

"Why don't you just go sit in the common room," replied the firm, stony mouth of Stacey.

My questions remained unanswered, yet my head was full of more to ask. A never-ending artillery of questions lay on my tongue. Clashing thoughts could only be resolved by answers, answers to more *questions!*

"Are there lots of teenagers in the common room?" I asked, unstoppable in my quest for answers.

I was obedient to her commands concerning the common room, yet I remained attached to my unsubtle methods of detective work concerning Elena. I could never obey completely.

"Are the teenagers in the common room ones who dropped out of school?"

"They did not drop out of school."

"Oh," I sighed, feeling that Stacey's stony exterior would shatter, giving way to angry lava. "Are the teenagers in the common room like me? People who are smart, yet got expelled because they didn't fit in with other teenagers at school? They did not drop out?"

I realised I had tested her enough.

"Why don't you go and find out," she said sharply, walking away from me.

Watching Stacey leave for the staff room, I noticed how tightly, above that grey stone face, how tightly her thin, black hair was pulled up into a bun. Her scalp seemed almost to be screaming out in pain. Her leggings were also tight, riding up against her thick calves, straining against her round belly. They would leave a red tide-mark when she took them off, I thought. The T-shirt she wore was printed with a smiley face and the slogan: "DON'T WORRY! BE HAPPY!" Maybe she was a P.E. teacher after all. She wore trainers and had an air of stern authority about her. Perhaps I had offended her by mentioning missing her chosen teaching subject.

Music hummed monotonously, rather than blared, from behind a sterile white door. Opening it, I was greeted by what looked like the drawing of a very young child hung upon the opposite wall. The picture showed a smiling stick-girl. Above the white horizon of unfilled paper lay a line of blue sky, the sun hanging down like a large yellow blister.

Beneath the artwork sat a tall, lanky boy with closely cropped black hair. Slightly older than myself, and dressed casually, he stared heavenward, as if caught in a dream.

Taking the chance to approach the dreamer, I introduced myself: "Hi. I'm Jessica. What do they call you?"

No reply.

Slightly offended by his ignoring me, I persisted: "Did your little brother or sister draw that picture?"

No reply.

"Do you have a brother or sister? Did they send you that picture?"

No reply. Maybe he was lost in thought, or maybe he was just a loner like I was.

An uncomfortable silence enshrouded the both of us as I felt my resolve of politeness slip.

"Hey!" I said loudly, tapping his shoulder. "Hey! Who drew it then?"

"Me..." he said, drawling the word as "muy". Repeating the single word, he began to crack his fingers together. Nerves, I thought.

"That's funny!" I laughed with unease. "You sound just like Stig of the Dump!"

"Muy...Muy!" he continued, beginning to rock backwards and forwards. Rock and crack, rock and crack.

"What's your *real* name, Stig?" I laughed, trying hard to look into his eyes.

"Muy...Muy!"

"What IS your name?" I began to grow frustrated with his little game.

"Muy..." He held out his hand to shake mine with great force, almost crushing my fingers. "Muy Juno-fhun."

Suddenly, he reeled forwards before clapping his huge palms together in my face. A grin spread from one cheek to the other revealing straight, white teeth.

Stepping backwards, I could not help but stare as I observed his strange movements. Juno-fhun certainly had a bizarre sense of humour.

"Juno-fhun! Juno-fhun!" he laughed. "Muy, muy gudmurnin! Gudmurnin fafternoon."

"It's not a good morning *or* afternoon," I sighed. "It's too bright and too cold."

"Gudmurnin! Gud fafternoon!" he persisted, holding out his enormous digits in my direction. "Wush curs! Wush curs!"

Was he wanting to wash cars?

"Wun wush curs," he began to imitate a sponge being wiped across a car roof.

"See you later, Juno-fhun. Enjoy washing cars."

I could see why Juno-fhun had been expelled. Obviously, he had been the class joker and still liked to speak in tongues. Imagining him writing his essays in that German-caveman dialect, he probably created other fantastic hybrids of language as humour. Juno-fhun, if that was his real name, had probably drawn the stick-girl himself, handing over the credit to some imaginary younger sibling.

"Wush curs! WUSH CURS!" he bellowed across the room.

"Later, Jonathan," said an assistant. "It's a little cold, don't you think?"

Jonathan picked up a book, flicking over the pages at lightspeed as opposed to reading them. He was performing an act of defiance. Looking closely at the cover, it was a "Postman Pat" book. Obviously not a fan of children's literature, he threw it to the floor in a temper.

Rebellious and full of wild humour, he struck me as being little more than a big kid.

Glancing over towards the patch of carpet cleared as a dance floor, I saw several differently sized, differently clothed clones indulging in what seemed to be the same dance. Their moves were identical, if not particularly graceful. Their dance involved rocking sideways, from one foot to the other, but always in perfect time to the music. This must be the new school craze, I thought, debating with myself whether to join them.

Without warning, an attractive, curly-haired boy, who closely resembled the actor Fred Savage, aeroplaned through the crowd towards me. Arms flailing, legs bending akimbo, he reeled through the bodies with a venomous gleam in his eye. Focusing on the figure cutting a path through the swaying, dancing human forest, I caught him in my glance. He was beautiful! Olive skin framing features of perfect masculine beauty, he would be the target of my affections. Smiling to myself, I knew that here was a reason to stay at Easton House.

"Lang-a-lang-a-LIIIIIING!" he hollered, felling a nearby dancer to the floor.

A Red Indian war-cry! This boy was into role-play. He was warning off all the competition! Enthralled, I watched him smash a girl to the floor with his arm. Rising slowly, she whimpered before rejoining the tribal dance.

"LANG-a-lang-a-LIIIIIING!" he hollered again, yet louder, more free and unrestrained.

Taken by his dramatic, if violent, performance, I sidled up beside him, casually swinging my hips to the music of the stereo.

"Hi. I'm Jessica," I said seductively, barely controlling the grin that had blossomed across my face.

No reply. This boy just *had* to dance! He was playing hard to get and needed a little persuasion.

"Hi. Been tearing up the dance floor like this all your life?"

Still he danced. My line fell on absent ears.

"So, man of mystery, who *are* you?"

"LANG-a-lungalunga-LIIING!"

"Oh. Are you…er, foreign?" I was shaken by the shrill, cacophonous nature of his words. Surely no human language could sound quite like that. Something was wrong.

Reeling around, he continued his caterwauling.

"I'm English. Not proud of it, mind," I laughed, nervously. "Please speak to me if you know how."

Unable to reply in anything resembling dialogue, he howled and screeched until a boy in the corner placed his hands over his ears. Giving up, I sat down, deafened and confused.

"That's Richie," explained an assistant. "He's non-verbal."

"He's lovely," I sighed. "But what's this non-verbal business?"

"Richie can't talk or phrase sentences," she explained. "Instead, he uses a book to communicate with people."

"A book, huh?" I opened my eyes in surprise. "So he's mute? Noisy, but mute? And he can read, but not talk, right?"

"Half-right," said the assistant.

Her hair was long and fell into auburn curls across her shoulders. She was enviably much prettier than me, I noticed with a pang of despair. However, I was taller by an inch, and probably heavier. I could take her in a fight if she depressed me too much.

"Half-right?" I continued the conversation. "So I could write him a letter and he would write one back?"

"No. He needs dots to write with. He can't read words, just recognise pictures."

"Then how come he has a plastic book tagged onto his jeans?" At first, I had thought the object was merely an elaborate keyring.

"That is a book of signs, of pictures. Richie points at a picture from the book with his finger to show what he wants. A symbol of a jug means he wants orange juice."

"Richie is so handsome," I sighed with a smile. "It's a shame he can't talk."

"We all wish that," nodded the assistant. "By the way, I'm Jeanette."

"I'm Jessica. I'm thirteen. Are you a teacher?"

"No," replied Jeanette, her eyes unnaturally large and blue, not sunken and brown like mine, "I work as a care assistant."

"What do care assistants do? Do they care, like the Care Bears, or just assist?"

"We look after the young people in this building." As she dropped the words 'look after' from her tongue, they jarred ominously against her full, pink lips.

"*Why* can't Richie talk?" I asked, with a single-mindedness I was swiftly growing proud of.

"Nobody knows, not even Richie. Richie, like all of the young people in this building, has autism."

Unaware of this condition named *autism*, I leapt without a pause to my defence: "I don't have autism! I have Asparagus, sorry, Asperger's syndrome!"

"Asperger's syndrome is a higher functioning variant of autism." Jeanette's words could have been read from the page of a doctor's textbook!

I glared at her. She avoided my eyes.

"Do you know what Asperger's syndrome is?"

"Yes. It just means that I'm a rebellious loner who has up-and-down moods and..." I paused, "I lose my temper occasionally. I'm sensitive. I cry a lot. But I can talk perfectly well." I paused again. "I get good grades, mind you. I write good stories. I get As and Bs for them in English class." I was going nowhere. Pausing for over a minute, I blurted out: "Who's your favourite pop group?"

Unemotionally, she nodded: "I like lots of music. I don't have a favourite pop group."

"I like Duran Duran!" I said, unaware of the overt enthusiasm in my voice. "John Taylor, the bass-player, is my favourite. He's gorgeous! Those hazel eyes, those cheekbones! He's so tall and so sexy! What would you do if he walked into this room right this minute?"

"I don't know," she pondered, uninterested. "I know you'd do something."

"Yeah! I'd run away with him in his Ferrari."

"Surely you don't want to run away from Easton House when you've just moved in? It's very nice here."

The word *nice* added an artificial saccharine touch to her sentence. I had already decided that I did not like this woman.

"I'm not staying here. I don't like *nice* and I don't have autism!" The words spat themselves from my lips.

Rising swiftly, I strode towards the door. Before the exit stood a flush-faced, authoritarian figure. Clad in a long, floral, Laura Ashley-style frock, she appeared, from a distance, to be in late middle age. The hair was short and tightly curled: the sort of mousy-brown locks possessed only by librarians, dowagers and spinsters. Suddenly, I stopped.

"Hello! I'm Sally!" she sang, her voice shrill yet audible. This one could talk!

Her face was round-cheeked, innocent, almost cherubic. Half child, half librarian, I found myself thinking of a collage of Victorian Christmas cards and the bygone days of war widows studying that idyll. This amalgamated image was soon shattered with another blast of that sing-song voice.

"Hello! I like you!"

"Hello, Sally. Do you know anything about autism?"

"I don't...don't know," she trilled. "Do you like Simon and Garfunkel? Do you? DOOO YOUUU?"

"No!" I snapped, "I think they're a load of crap! What *is* bloody autism?"

"Bloody and crap are rude words," sang Sally, offended. "*Jeanette! Jeanette!* This lady is using rude words!"

"Sally doesn't like you using that language, and neither do I," scolded the mechanical Jeanette.

"Sally just used the words herself," I replied smartly in my defence.

"She repeats things," explained the pretty android. "Sally is echolalic. It is not wise to swear in front of her."

"But I bet *you* swear in the house. Everybody does – even the Pope!"

"Maybe he does, but nobody swears here."

"I just did, albeit mildly."

"I don't like to swear!" chorused Sally, pushing in front of me. "I don't LIKE to swear! Swearing is rude! Swearing is silly! Swearing is naughty!"

The word *naughty* came straight from an Enid Blyton book. Maybe the archaic, yet young, Sally had been expelled for being a blast from the past.

"I don't want to swear! I don't WANT to be silly! I don't WANT TO BE NAUGHTY!" she shrieked, her song now falling out of tune. "Am I being sensible? Am I? AM I?"

"Sally, read a book," ordered Jeanette.

Picking up Postman Pat, Sally gazed at the pictures with a blankness stretched across her face.

"Silly girl! SILLY GIRL!" she sang, "I don't WANT to be a silly girl!"

"Sally. Don't repeat," said Jeanette with another warning. "You don't want to be a Polly Parrot."

"Polly Parrot! POLLY PARROT!"

"What *is* autism?" I asked, unappeased and desperate.

"Ask the teachers. I'm going for my break."

– TWO –

"STACEY!"

Finally, I cornered her in the classroom.

"Stacey!" I hollered, exasperated. "What is autism?"

"Autism is a registered disability," she replied smugly – another textbook Methodist.

"But I'm not disabled!" I protested. "Look: two legs! I can walk. Two eyes! I can see!"

"No. Autism is not a physical disability," she corrected me.

"Then it's a mental one," I guessed. "I knew it. I'm mental."

"Calm down. You are not mental."

I remembered my non-too-distant days at school: "Everybody used to say that I was mental, but I'm not mental. I've just got Asparagus syndrome, and that'll heal. I'll get better. I'm not as mad as half the people here, so therefore I must be normal. Normal. Not mad. Sane."

"What you have is Asperger's syndrome." Her eyes never moved as her mouth recited the line.

"I know!" My air became haughtier in my defiance. "So I shouldn't be here, in THIS place with all these mad autism people. I don't have autism and I'm definitely not mad, so I *must* be normal. I shall pack my suitcase, ring Mum and go home. Then I can go to a normal school, with normal people who can talk properly. This place depresses me. I want to go home."

"If you go back home, you won't learn anything," came the warning.

"Yes I will!" Standing, hands on hips, like the King of Siam, I retorted: "I can go back to a normal school and get good grades like I used to. Anyway, I want to be with girls my own age who I can make friends with: normal, talky girls. Girls who talk like me and listen to pop music! Gimme the phone! I'm ringing my mum. My Mum'll get me out of this place."

"I thought you were expelled," mused Stacey, stone teeth smiling a slate smile.

"I wasn't," I continued, raising my voice over the murmuring behind me. "I was unjustly exiled! I can go back any time I want."

Seating myself on a sticky plastic chair, I adopted the forlorn stance of a refugee. Gazing upwards into her unblinking, bespectacled eyes, I wrung my hands with deep anxiety.

The classroom was small, confined in a tiny box of wallpapered plaster. It jarred somewhat with the huge French window and its view of freedom. Looking out over the overgrown garden, I spied, behind the tangled mesh of rose bushes, the welcoming tarmac of the road. However, needing my questions answered, I decided to stay put.

Around the walls hung various uninteresting maps and charts. Ignoring these, I studied the gallery of crudely drawn pictures, presumably drawn by the *young people*. Vainly, I imagined my own creations up there in contrast. Priding myself as an artist, I knew that my reproduction of Duran Duran's *Rio* album cover would shine against the competition.

"Lang-a-lang-a-LIIIIIING!"

Stacey pointed Richie outside the classroom. We were having a private talk.

"See! I'm not like *him*," I stated. "I shouldn't be in this place. It's like the Addams Family here!"

"No," came the witness for the defence of Easton House. "It is like a pleasant home full of young people with autism."

"Except me," I said, predictably.

Folding my arms in my lap, I abdicated from my defiant throne. Clumsily, I whispered: "Can I get expelled from this place?"

"Nobody is expelled from Easton House. We are all patient here."

"Patient…like a…hospital," I sang, knowing I was losing this battle.

Stacey let my sea of singing wash over her tightly bound scalp.

"Yeah. This place is a fucking hospital. Worse: it's a fucking loony-bin!"

"Please don't swear."

"Ooops! Sorry, I forgot that swearing was illegal. So I'm a fucking criminal now? This place is a prison."

Ignoring my swearing voice, Stacey began to write up some notes.

"Are you some sort of fucking secretary?"

"No. I am a qualified teacher."

Again, I rose: "You LOOK like a secretary! With your hair all tied up and those stupid glasses and that fucking writing pad!"

"Jessica. Keep your opinions to yourself. I'm not interested."

Sulkily, I wandered towards the window. Staring outside, I sighed deeply before wistfully pacing the circumference of the table.

"Relax," ordered Stacey, chewing her pen.

Decidedly unrelaxed, I continued to pace.

"Are there any normal girls here, like me, who I can talk to and make friends with?"

"Have you spoke to Sally yet?"

"Yes, but she's mad. Jesus! I can't relate to these people!"

On impulse, I began to cry with frustration. Tears had, throughout my life, been a method of self-defence rather than of pretence. If I was seen crying, my instincts told me, I would not have more insult added to injury. Tasting the salt in my mouth, I wrung a flaky tissue from my pocket before burying it in the bin.

"Have you met Shaun yet?"

"No. But he's a *boy*. I want to talk to girls as friends."

"Give him a chance," suggested Stacey, shrugging her shoulders.

As I decided to temporarily surrender, I found myself asking where the Shaun-boy was to be found. I was told he was playing chess in the room next door. To play chess, I thought, you had to be intelligent. Shaun might be a boy, but he could be on a similar intellectual level to my own.

I walked through the open door slowly. Underneath a large, mis-shapen collage of badly drawn figures, each representing a resident *young person*, was printed the slogan: "OUR FRIENDS AT EASTON HOUSE". Beneath the vividly papered letters various autographs had been scrawled. Tempted to add my own, I feared doing so would merely sign my contract of eternal confinement. I might be trapped for ever behind these scrawled-upon walls. I closed my eyes and imagined being transformed into a doodle, looking through the windows of a paper house. Watching cardboard cars drive past, down streets of streaky black paint, I would wonder why some people were drawn better than others.

Richie would be a stick man: photocopied dots forming the skeleton of his smudged crayon body. Sally would be a badly glued montage: the eyes and mouth not quite matching. Stacey, I thought, would be a newspaper cut-out: several shades of grey blending into one larger shape.

Beneath the chartreuse "F" of "FRIENDS" sat a hunched figure dressed all in black. Like a monochrome figure in an old photograph, colour seemed to be absent from his very being. His black polo-neck contrasted with his pale face, making it look almost white, tinged with the graphite shadows of stubble. His hair, cut short and plastered greasily to his forehead, was a mousy blond. It too seemed streaked with grey. He had the look of a beatnik about him. Against the absurdly bright backdrop, he brought a note of visual cynicism to the room.

Once standing, the figure was scarcely taller than I was. Broad-shouldered and stocky towards becoming cubical, he resembled the Man From U.N.C.L.E. gone to seed.

Moving a knight across the chessboard, I saw that he had no opponent. Capturing his own black bishop, he placed it in the limbo of his pocket.

"You must be very bored," I sighed, observing the look of nonchalance on his square-jawed face.

"Yeah," he replied in perfect, if monotone, English, "I'm just trying to look like I'm busy."

"Are you Shaun?"

"Yes. I'm Shaun Everett Rogers."

His was an impressive title, like that of a long-dead movie star. In truth, it suited him. He looked like a dead man talking.

"I'm Jessica Peers. My middle name's so secret, in truth it's boring."

"I thought you'd wear glasses," remarked Shaun, observing me. "I was told by Neil that you were brainy."

Shrugging off the cliché, I seated myself beside the chessboard. We looked out of place together in the corner, like a couple of absent art students.

"I'm thirteen."

"I'm eighteen," sighed Shaun. "I've not got long left here."

Stacey left the neighbouring classroom. It was time for her break. For a small period of time, the classrooms were empty of staff altogether.

"A-ha!" grinned Shaun, a flicker of light spanning his monochrome face. "It's time I got out the Big Book."

"The *Big Book*?" I asked, not really imagining him as the Biblical type.

"Simon!" he called with great urgency, his whisper breaking into almost a shout.

Bounding into the room came his accomplice in crime. Simon had the widest grin I had seen since my arrival, his face lit up by the neon keys of his face. Tanned and lanky, he seemed to burst like a beanstalk from his Teenage Mutant Ninja Turtles T-shirt. Hoisting up his jogging bottoms, comically high until they scaled his armpits, he greeted me in his broad Yorkshire accent.

"Aye-aye! I'm Peter Samson," he said, zealously shaking my hand.

Despite using a false name, which I suspected to be that of another *young person*, he was open and friendly. The contrast between these two figures – the stolid Shaun and the leaping, colourful Simon – was like bright paint on a blank canvas.

"Get out the book," urged Shaun.

Reaching behind the bookcase, Simon heaved out a volume so large its cracked spine seemed in a struggle to contain its pages. The front cover was missing so it appeared yet more taboo to its readers: faceless, anonymous, tempting. Catching a page number, I read the true title of this behemoth: *The Chronicle of the Twentieth Century*. Despite being abusively revered, the book was obviously educational.

"September first, nineteen fifty-two," requested Shaun as Simon selected the page in question.

A black and white photograph showed a small biplane engulfed in a cloud of thick, black smoke.

"Don Campbell's plane ploughed into the crowd," read Shaun, with wry interest.

I glanced down at the tragedy, strangely unmoved.

"Loads o' smoke on that picture!" laughed Simon, oblivious to the reality of the event. "Just like Bond films!"

Shaun smiled before selecting another disaster. Again, he lapped it up.

Before long, I discovered Shaun's other passion, aside from tragedy: James Bond. Complaining that the staff had confiscated his Ian Fleming novels, original 1960s editions, he had wondered if the staff had secretly burned them.

"There goes Ian Fleming's name in smoke," he had lamented. "I.A.N. F.L.E.M.I.N.G., like smoke signals."

Simon laughed, amused by the wit of Shaun.

Simon was soon revealed as being a few months younger than myself and keen on cars, tractors and computer games. Despite being a loud-talking, vivacious character, he held his own aspect of mystery. Instead of telling where he lived, he would just shrug and say: "Down the lane."

Grinning his familiar megawatt grin, Simon would enthuse about his Uncle Ernie and younger brother, Dan.

"*Casino Royale* wasn't a proper Bond movie," explained Shaun to the loyal Simon. "Instead of the usual star trilogy of Sean Connery, Roger Moore or even Timothy Dalton, they used David Niven as the actor to play Bond. Mind you, George Lazenby played Bond once, but never repeated the role. In *Casino Royale*, not proper Bond you understand, the irony is that there are over fifty 007s including...a woman! I would not class *Casino Royale* as a member of the Bond franchise. I would, however, class it as a spoof. Quite an entertaining spoof with good use of irony.

"*Dr No*, however, is a different matter altogether. A *real* Bond movie."

Shaun almost smiled as film titles began to leap from his mouth.

Suddenly, he turned to me and asked: "What do you think of Timothy Dalton?"

"Hmmm," I pondered. "I suppose he's still relatively young, and easy on the eye. Roger Moore's past it, mind you. His skin's like crimplene and I'm sure that's a wig he wears."

"Would you say that he was wooden?"

"So wooden he creaks," I replied, remembering the tedium I had experienced at Christmas during a repeat showing of *For Your Eyes Only*.

"I think he is definitely the blandest Bond," stated Shaun knowingly. He had probably had this conversation many times before with Simon. "I would say that since *Live and Let Die* he's never took an acting lesson. In the later Bonds, he was lagging even more. I think he was fifty-seven in *A View to A Kill*, probably the same age as David Niven in *Casino Royale*. I would say he looked closer to seventy and had not improved his technique. Seeing Moore in bed with women old enough to be his grandchildren makes me feel slightly uneasy, yet I would not say no if I was his age and had nubile young women offering themselves to me."

"Simon!" called the intrusive voice of Stacey. "Simon, come here a minute."

"Coming," muttered Simon, losing his glow.

"Have you been taking tapes from other people's drawers again?"

"No," pleaded Simon, voice quivering with guilt.

"What are these in my hands then?"

Holding out her hands, Stacey produced two Kylies and a *Party Hits 1985*.

"Tapes," stated the worried Simon. "I didn't take them."

"Who did then?" demanded Stacey.

"Peter Samson," explained Simon.

"Are you *sure*?"

"Yeah. Peter Samson took them."

"And I suppose Peter Samson stole those videos from the common room too."

"Yeah, he did. Peter Samson steals *everything*!"

"Then why were they all in the drawer that said *Simon Hirst*?"

"That's not my name!" protested Simon.

"Whose name is it then?"

"Peter Samson's name. He stole it!"

Rising to her full, terrible stature, Stacey sounded the alarm of her voice.

A dirty-blond boy of fifteen entered the room. Wearing a torn Michael Jackson T-shirt, I supposed he must be the legendary Peter Samson. Seating himself on a chair, he began humming T.V. themes to himself. Catching the melody of *Stingray*, I listened to the notes of his slightly abrasive voice.

"Peter," quizzed Stacey, "did you steal these tapes?"

"No," said Peter, looking up. He soon reverted back to the tune of *Stingray.*

"See, Simon. Peter didn't steal those tapes."

"Well *I* didn't steal them!" protested Simon.

Still pleading his case, Simon was led towards a jigsaw puzzle. Tipping the pieces onto the floor, Stacey gave him the task of reassembling them.

"No Ribena, Simon, until you've done your puzzle," she scolded as Peter was released.

Once she had turned her back, Simon threw one piece behind the wastepaper bin before putting another in his pocket. Poor Rosie and Jim would never be united fully.

In the corner sat Richie, joining up a numberless dot-to-dot kitten.

"Is there anybody normal here?" I asked Shaun, once again trapped by my own desperation.

"I don't know. There's Simon, but he's a bit funny."

"But he's your best mate."

"He does cool things," said Shaun, trying and failing to smile. "There's Neil, but he's a poser and a sex-fiend. There was Brownie, but he left before you came." Pausing, he looked me in the eye: "You're too normal for this place."

"I know," I sighed, realising the bookshelf stocked no Stephen King, only children's books. "There's just kids' stuff here, apart from your Big Book, of course."

"Yeah," complained Shaun. "They took away all my Bond books. They took another of my favourite books: *She* by H. Rider Haggard. I bought it from Cat Concern. I like the film. It stars Ursula Andress, also known as Honey Ryder from *Dr No.* She's sexually active on a scale of eight out of ten."

"*Sexually active? Out of ten?*" I got his game: he was rating people on their sexual attractiveness! "What would you give Stacey then? Out of ten?"

"Oh, just a two. If that. What would you give her?"

"The same. What marks would you give Margaret Thatcher?"

"One out of sympathy."

This game of sex and numbers was quickly becoming highly addictive. Within the space of five minutes we had raced through various celebrities: Phil Collins (two), John Taylor (eleven hundred!), Roger Moore (two, but nought-point-five for acting ability), Jeremy Beadle (minus six-hundred-and-sixty-six). Simon scored a seven, just for being Shaun's best mate.

"What music do you like?" I suddenly asked him. "I like Duran Duran."

"Oh, I quite like Duran Duran, a bit. I once bought *Rio* from a car boot sale. Simon Le Bon looks like he's on drugs in the video to *Planet Earth*. My favourite bands are…er," here came the pause before the enthusiasm. "I sort of like The Fortunes, The Seekers, The Tremoloes, The 1910 Fruitgum Co. Sixties music."

"Are you a Beatnik?"

"I don't know," he replied indecisively.

A moment of silence passed between us. Staff walked into the room and Shaun felt uncomfortable. He was rather like a spy, not wishing to pass on information to the wrong people. I soon learned that he rarely spoke when they were around, giving the appearance of somebody unusually quiet. Like a human statue, he remained silent and solemn, only occasionally turning to whisper in my ear a snippet concerning *The New Avengers* or *Randall and Hopkirk, Deceased*.

Handed a textbook, I protested that the work was too easy. Frowning, Stacey put my name down for French. Uninspired, I answered each mundane question. Scrawling down one answer with my eyes shut, I mocked the textbook.

As I was sat mocking, a tall, bespectacled man wandered carefree into the room. Whistling an old Bob Dylan song, he rattled the keys in his pocket. Strolling up to the desk, which I shared with Shaun, he greeted me.

"Hi. You must be Jessica," he smiled casually. "I'm Vincent. I'm in charge of drama and all things dramatic."

Suddenly, I found myself liking Vincent's style.

"We're doing a play this year," he added. "Actually, it's just our usual Christmas pantomime, but this year I thought it could be something quite special. We're doing *Alice in Wonderland*, but with some of my own added humour."

Shaun whispered in my ear. I heard something about drugs, white rabbits and Jefferson Airplane.

At school, despite being good at drama off the stage, my dreams of a starring role had often been shattered due to my more popular class-mates getting the best roles. My name was usually pushed to second-from-bottom where the Christmas Cabaret was concerned. My simplest role had been in *The Twelve Days of Christmas*, simple enough even for Roger Moore to act with panache. Holding aloft a large cardboard sign I had drawn myself, I read out the legend "TWELVE DRUMMERS DRUMMING" in a clear voice.

Before that, my short and unvaried stage career had involved playing a Russian dancer in an over-simplified *Baboushka*, reading out three lines as Cook in *The Stepping Stone*, and taking the part of narrator several times. Usually this latter role involved reading the unmemor-able middle-section in assembly.

I lost out many times due to my inability to sing. Dad had no qualms telling me to quit any singing ambitions. I knew my voice was bad. However, my reading voice was always good. I knew how to make it carry towards the back of the room.

"We're looking for an Alice," offered Vincent. "Originally, we were going to choose Anita, but she preferred to be the Voice of Lewis Carroll."

Vincent was like a genie offering me my wish of a starring role! Stunned, I thought of the offer. Although Alice had always struck me as a slightly bland, dipsy character, I was willing to take on my first leading role. Smiling to myself, I realised there would be little acting involved. After all, I could identify with the bewildered Alice. Cast astray in a surreal world full of bizarre characters, her questions never truthfully answered, Alice was not at all unlike myself. Maybe Vincent had observed these parallels.

"Will I have to wear a daft frock?" I asked, questioning the draw-backs.

"I'm afraid you will," apologised Vincent. "But the rest of the cast will look far sillier. They'll be dressed as rabbits, caterpillars and mad flowers. Very silly indeed!"

"Cool. I'll take the part," I agreed.

My stay in Wonderland now had a sense of purpose.

– THREE –

IMPATIENTLY, I WAITED in the queue for the girls' bathroom. Swaddled in my swiftly unravelling dressing-gown, I felt the shame of my hairy legs. Glancing in front of myself, however, I observed that other legs, too, were unshaven. Guided out from the bathroom came a slim, blonde girl, her long hair being gently combed by Jeanette. Like a movie star, she appeared impeccable, immaculate, even when wet and bare-faced. Consoling myself with the fact that the girl's lips were rather thin, I stared over with envy.

"This is Calista Smith. She'll be sharing a bedroom with you."

"Oh."

"She's quite quiet and well behaved. I think you two will get along fine."

As Calista was led to her pampering session, I wondered why it was she who got the special attention. As I had done to my sister's Barbie dolls in the past, I imagined dyeing her hair purple with mascara and giving her a rude tattoo.

Elena entered the bathroom, struggling against the arms that guided her. Whimpering loudly, she tore open her dressing-gown, revealing a body painfully thin. Modestly, I looked away. Suddenly, she bit hungrily into the fleshless bone of her shoulder, drawing blood from the deep, circular scar that blossomed there. Violently, the staff member was thrown against the wall. Running fast, Jeanette came to her assistance.

Holding down Elena was a large, red-haired woman, her florid face filled with concern. Together, the two women tried to aid her through the unlocked door.

"Eunice! Get Eva!" called Jeanette, struggling for breath as her winded companion was left in control.

Eva Pearson, skin like a scorched tangerine, nuclear blonde hair rising in immaculate curls above her sportswear-clad shoulders, ran to the rescue. Her trainer-padded footsteps fell lightly in contrast to the clomping strides of Eunice.

Shrill weeping could be heard from behind the bathroom door. Deep, irregular gulps and gurgles punctuated the weeping. The door remained locked.

As a *responsible* girl, I had been expected to wait at the back of the queue. I would like to have felt sympathy for the crouched figure behind the door, but instead I felt pity. Elena could fight back physically to no avail; the staff would give her a worse punishment. She could not complain vocally for they had probably heard the same words, the same groans and gurgles before. Rather selfishly, the sense of pity was a side-effect of my own feelings of superiority. I was fully *verbal*, a *normal* human being. She was unable to control her voice or her body.

Despite these mixed feelings, I was frustrated by a purely physical need: the need to be clean, the need to have a bath and wash my hair. Inside me, the frustration grew until I could feel bacteria crawling across my scalp, running down my thighs and over the downy surface of my arms. Desperation made me screw my face up, grit my teeth, twist the cable of my dressing-gown.

Time hobbled by to the sound of a distant television set, most of the programmes worth missing. As each manic, yet lethargic, minute passed I found myself tearing the wood chip from the walls, small splinters wedging themselves beneath my nails. Soon a hole had made an appearance in the wallpaper and a cut had opened on my finger. Unravelling a string of cotton from my pyjamas, I twisted it into a knot. A spider-sized cat's cradle began to form itself in my palm.

After half an hour Elena made her exit, leaving behind both her towel and her dressing-gown. Glancing sideways in the opposite direction as she was ordered to retrieve the garments, I rooted in my toilet-bag for my shampoo. Quickly, I rose and set my things down by the bath. Suddenly, horrified, I drew back. The door, I noticed, had NO LOCK!

Freezing on the tiles, I searched in disbelief for anything at all resembling that great defender of privacy. I found nothing.

I called Eva. Eva laughed at me. There was definitely *no* lock, nor had there ever been. Devastated, I hung my head and shed a few tears. Eva ignored me and walked away. In a moment of hope, I placed a chair against the door. Eva told me not to. I began to panic.

"No hairwash unless you stop these hysterics!"

The panic grew worse. At this moment, as rage began to gather inside my chest, I found myself hating Eva.

Sweating and angered, I struggled with both Eva and myself. Above it all rose the negotiator: a part of me that strode away from the Jessica on the battlefield.

"I'll stop panicking," I said, breathing in a gust of air, "on condition that when I go in the bath nobody else goes in the bathroom. If anyone sees my flab, I'm allowed to kick them out, right?"

"We don't tolerate that kind of attitude here," she frowned. "Just get in the bath with no complaints."

Behind the door, once she was out of sight, I found myself whispering the words "heartless bitch".

Slyly, I blocked the entrance with my dressing-gown and towel. Washing my hair, I finally felt at ease, until Sally used her massive arms to burst through the blockade, wiping her red, sweaty face on my towel. Yelling at her, I sent the intruder back down the corridor.

Upon hearing the uproar, Eva came running. Omnipotent, Eva was both anywhere and everywhere at the same time. Perhaps there was an entire army of Evas roaming around Easton House in search of people to be punished. Reluctantly greeting *this* Eva, I was cautioned with a shampoo confiscation.

"You shall have to use soap, Jessica!"

Weeping heartily, I skulked gracelessly towards my bedroom. Greeted eagerly by the smiling face of John Taylor and his comrades, my mood lightened slightly. There was still hope in my dreams. Looking down at me from his place on the wall, paper face both handsome and compassionate, his long-lashed hazel eyes seemed to understand my pain. Had he been there at that moment, he would surely have sneaked me out through a window and into his waiting Ferrari. Gingerly, I dried my hair, eyes forever drifting towards his revered visage.

Calista sat opposite me on the right-hand side of the room. I was on the left. Long blonde hair flowing, freshly dried over her slim shoulders, she looked more like the princess whom John Taylor would rescue. I was plain. Reaching for an expensive-looking brush, she lovingly smiled to herself in the mirror. Glancing at my drying hair from behind her, I could see she wanted me out of her limelight.

On going to sleep that night there was no conversation. Calista seemed uninterested in anything I said, not even bringing herself to reply. Eventually, I shut my big mouth.

Rolling beneath the friendly duvet, I pulled it over my head. Closing my red-rimmed eyes, I lapsed slowly into John Taylor's embrace.

— FOUR —

MY JEANS WERE washed once a week. That was normal, or so it was to me. Unaware that most people washed their clothes more often, I thought I was truly upholding my own strict laws of cleanliness: I washed my hands after the toilet or after touching anything I thought to be dirty, washed my face several times a day and made sure that my nails were not brown. My hair was washed once a week, due to Mum's insistence that it was healthier to do so that way.

Today my jeans had dust on their knees, but I knew to wash them at the end of the week: on Fridays. Overhearing that clothes at Easton House were washed daily, or every two days, I began to re-think my principles.

"My jeans aren't dirty, are they?" I asked Eva, my mind filled with doubt.

"They're not dirty." For a moment I was relieved. "They're *filthy*."

"I'm NOT dirty!" I protested, knowing myself that I was wrong.

"If you think you're not dirty," frowned Eva, "then you can keep those jeans on all week *without* washing them."

Turmoil. I had lost my principles AND those principles had been proven wrong. I was lost: a loser in both cases, *and my jeans were filthy*.

Knowing I had lost, I fought back anyway. It was the only way I knew.

Standing defiantly, I yelled: "If you think my fucking jeans are dirty, then you can bloody well wash them! If everybody else's jeans get washed daily, SO CAN MINE!"

"You've already lost that opportunity," scolded Eva. "You shall wear your dirty jeans."

"I can wear other clothes!" I rebelled.

"If you do," she threatened, "you shall go to your room and change back into your dirty jeans."

No way out. Choosing to be as far from my tormentor as possible, I hot-footed it towards the door. Eva caught me in mid-stride with her tangerine arm.

"You're not going anywhere."

"I AM! I'm getting out of here!"

Struggling against her grip, I broke free and ran towards the stairs, passing Eunice on the way. Finally, I reached the front door. To my despair, it was locked! Behind me, I could hear the heavy tread of Eunice accompanied by the dainty steps of Jeanette. I was lifted from the floor and dragged back up the stairway. Above me, I saw the grinning face of the toxic Eva.

"Duvet her!"

Duvet? A duvet was something you slept under, wasn't it? What did punishment have to do with a sleeping comfort? I was soon to find out.

A large, blue king-sized duvet was laid out flat upon the floor. I supposed I was to lie on top to calm down. Still fighting against the embrace of Eunice and Jeanette, I began to kick.

"Violence and aggression," stated Eva. "Lie her down."

Still I rebelled. Near breathless, I pushed each of their attempts away. Although outnumbered, I still believed I could run. Swiftly, I ducked, managing a few footsteps away from my captors. My legs were bowed beneath me as their arms took me once again. As my feet dragged against the door-stop, I was lifted, my elbows red from the locks of their fingers.

Thrown down onto the wide blue square, I noticed stains all around me. Although born without a sense of smell, I could tell by the colour that the stains were urine. Somebody had obviously lost control of their bladder whilst enduring this treatment. Trying to rise from a lying position, I was pushed back down onto the stained blue mess. My breath seemed to chug loudly from my lungs.

Then the duvet was rolled. I was being mummified. My arms and legs were by my sides, rolled up in this giant bandage. Strait-jacketed, I was laid on my front. Panic seized me as I found I was unable to move. Sweat and tears ran into my mouth and eyes. I was being drowned and suffocated at once.

Suddenly I felt a weight between my shoulders. My heart and lungs were crushed into my chest. My ribs felt as though they would break. Above me I could hear the voice of Eunice, big, heavy Eunice! Her words were swamped by the ringing in my ears. The chugging of my breath became a strangled wheezing.

Another weight landed on my legs, which were still kicking for freedom. This weight was lighter: Jeanette.

The final weight was the one that crushed. Eva sat on my face. My head was turned sideways in order to breathe. One cheek was engulfed by Eva, the other being burned against the carpet. The duvet wrapped itself higher as I writhed beneath the weights, covering my mouth, nose and eyes. Breathing was now impossible.

I could feel my cheek being fried by the heat of my damp sweat. The blindness and dumbness terrified me more than the inability to move my limbs. I was crippled.

With all my might, I let from my dry throat a cry of defiance. All air inside me was gone. I thought I was going to die. As I did so, I imagined the trio of torturers being led to court for manslaughter. Not reassured, I fell silent. Perhaps if I faked dying they would leave me. I was blowing it all out of proportion. They would never believe my act.

Finally I could see again. The weights slowly rose from my back and the duvet was unrolled. Shaking and panting, I was hoisted from my lying position. My legs felt like they had been run over by a train and my head felt hollow.

I felt dirty inside and out. My clothes would smell of my own sweat and the urine of others. My hair was glued to my head and soaked from its roots. As I walked to the bathroom, my heart beat faster than the music leaking from the radio.

– FIVE –

MEALTIMES WERE A place of worship at Easton House, each lasting one hour exactly. From the start to the finish, food was a ritual of great proportions. My refusal to drink coffee sparked disdain, as coffee was the sacrificial drink, and my dislike of gravy was heresy. Wishing to leave the table at teatime before the set ending was frowned upon. Stopped in my tracks at quarter to six, I was to endure the meal in its entirety.

The need of the staff for routine was greater than that of the young people. I found no point in sitting down after I had finished my portion. Deep inside, I knew I wolfed my food down, wished I could eat more slowly and precisely. As penance for finishing first, I was to sit staring as other people tucked in. Inside, I was hungry for more food. Eva often singled me out as the greedy one.

Kitchen duties were put on the nightly rota. Usually the more responsible young people were given these duties as they were less trouble for the staff to supervise. Not surprisingly, I was usually in this group. Not surprisingly, this was often a troublesome affair.

"Fuck you! Fuck the lot of you slave-drivers! If you talk to me like that again, I'll make sure you all suffer!"

"No, Jess. You cannot get out of kitchen duties," warned Eunice.

"Fat old ginger bitch!"

"Right," she retorted, face crimson against the red of her curls. "Instead of going to supper like the rest of us at eight-thirty, you shall stay down here and clean up after everyone."

After a long protest of curses and tears, I was frog-marched to the kitchen where a dire Aladdin's cave of pots and pans lay awaiting my services. On the draining board sat a leaning tower of saucepans and in the sink squatted the hideous remains of other people's enjoyment. Stomach empty and eyes stinging of salt, I felt very much like Cinderella, albeit a Cinderella who swore at staff and was fast developing a fear of the duvet.

My hands ached and throbbed as my precious nails were dashed to pieces. Weeping at their loss, I glanced dolefully at Eunice. Unforgiven, I received merely the glare of authority and another sinkful of exhaustion. Losing my nerve, I aimed a ladle at her head.

Sadly, I missed.

Instead of defeating the enemy, I had merely infuriated it. Eunice added a mop and bucket to the punishment. Now I felt more like the Sorcerer's Apprentice than Cinderella.

To the tune of *Here We Go Round the Mulberry Bush*, Eunice began to sing: "This is the way we mop the floor, mop the floor, mop the floor."

She had a bad voice.

Her red, grinning face infuriated me. Like a beacon of superiority, it shone down on my misery. Reaching for a large carving-knife, I held it nervously against my wrist. I wanted out. At that moment I told myself I wanted to die.

"I would rather die than be your slave," I said out loud.

"Put down the knife," sighed Eunice, tapping her big foot. "That doesn't work here."

Gathering my breath, I cried: "I am a woman of the WORLD, not a woman of the KITCHEN!"

For a moment, I felt like some brave suffragette. That moment soon ended as I realised that Eunice was completely unmoved by every one of my actions. Like a television on standby, she just stood and stared, empty yet commanding.

"Put down the knife and stop being silly!"

"I'm being serious. I'm a very serious person."

"So I've gathered. Stop this comedy right now."

"That's it!" I started. "Now I really *am* running away. If I can't get through that door, I really *will* kill myself!"

"Oh, really?" writhed Eunice with irony. "Wouldn't *that* be a shame."

Still holding the knife, I pelted down the corridor. Slamming shut the kitchen door, I heard the familiar heavy footsteps behind. Greasy hair obscured my vision. My limbs felt tired.

"This is the way we mop the floor, mop the floor, mop the floor…"

Placing my hands over my ears, I ran harder and faster. Knowing the door would be locked, I was still drawn to it. Like a moth to a lightbulb, I knew I was doomed, but kept on going.

Seconds later, with sore arms and a dry mouth, I was back in the kitchen. Eunice had taken the knife from me, replacing it with the hated mop. Reluctantly, I set to work on the already thrice-cleaned floor.

"It doesn't need another clean," I observed, bleary-eyed.

"That's not the point. You're on kitchen duties."

There was no escaping my fate when Eunice was supervising.

As the hours and minutes ticked by on the clock, my hands worked away on autopilot. Under the glare of the flickering halogen bar, the stainless steel draining board gradually emptied itself. The floor shone spotlessly, save for the deliberate prints of Eunice's feet. Occasionally, she would scrape her scuffed shoes against a patch I had already done.

As the clock hit ten and I had missed my precious hairwash, I was relieved of my sentence. To my astonishment, Eunice made me a cool glass of Ribena. To my even greater surprise, she allowed me to drink it. After that, I was released.

Eunice swallowed her pride and told me I had done a good job. By this I was shocked. I found myself laughing as she described how she hated kitchen duties as much as I did. Together, we agreed for once and walked together up the stairs for a biscuit.

− SIX −

"STINGRAY! STINGRAY! DER-DER-DER-DER-NER-NER!"

Peter Samson sat engulfed within the television world, its SuperMarionation cities and figures creating a new, more preferable reality.

Tapping his watch, he grinned: "STING-RAY on seven-o-clock."

A submarine lodged itself within a craggy plastic undersea cave. A gigantic squid, probably the size of a fist, entrapped it with its tentacles, pulling it further towards its simulated doom. Meanwhile, the hardy animated crew, becoming more heroic by the second, sounded the distress alarm. The signal rang out across the ocean, merging into the familiar theme tune.

Marina, mute and *non-verbal*, nodded her head with deep reverence as Stingray blasted herself through a cloud of bubbles.

"Mariiii-naaa! Aqua Mariiii-naaa!" sang the rapturous Peter, blowing kisses at his muse.

The squid lay mutilated, limbs flayed and severed by the blast of a laser cannon. The crew cheered with wild, wooden applause.

"*Stingray* on seven-o-clock-on-Mondays, *Thunderbirds* on seven-thirty-on-Thursdays," narrated Peter as the credits rolled. "*The Time Tunnel* on six-thirty-on-Fridays!"

"What else is on, Sammo?" I asked as he read the T.V. guide.

"*Lost In Space!*" he grinned in anticipation. "Saturday morning, ten-thirty!"

Reaching for a large bag of video tapes, he pulled out a selection of his favourites.

"*Thunderbirds*," he smiled, "*Lost In Space.*"

"Do you like *Terrahawks*?" I asked, having fond memories of the series from my younger days.

At school, I had once drawn a large, intricately detailed picture of my favourite character, Dr Tiger Ninestein. I had often wondered where he had earned the moniker of "Tiger" from, although "Ninestein" was obviously a suggestion of intelligence. I had also drawn the rest of the cast. Hawkeye, the young rookie pilot, had been my sister's favourite. Mary Falconer had been Ninestein's love interest, but she had been a little dull and no sparks had ever been truly ignited between the wooden couple. Kate Kestrel had been a pilot by day, pop singer by night. Her afro hair had changed its dayglo hue each episode. Zelda, the space-crone, had terrified Dad.

"*Terrahawks*," he mused. "Getting video from Dad next week."

I could wait. As consolation, Peter sang the entire theme tune, word for word, even ending with a loud "TERRAHAWKS! STAY ON THIS CHANNEL!".

"*Captain Scarlet!*" he pointed, showing me his old Gerry Anderson annuals. A picture of the Angels aroused interest in a passing male staff member and I swooned at a picture of the handsome Captain himself. Alerting my senses to a picture of the mature Colonel White, Peter pointed out: "That's Derek! Derek Dell!"

Commander Derek Dell was the houseparent, the senior of all staff. A tall, white-haired old gentleman, slowly becoming a veteran, he would walk into the common room with Bing Crosby on his lips and a biro in the top pocket of his crisply ironed C&A shirt. Perpetually forty-nine, he hummed and whistled away the years, sometimes clapping his hands to rouse the troops.

Pulling out a comb from his beige Farah slacks, he urged Peter Samson to sit up straight. Deftly, he parted the trooper's hair in a straight line to the right of his head. Swiftly moving over towards the reluctant Simon, hair encased in a sweaty Super Mario baseball cap, he failed to notice this trooper swipe his hair back into its original mop-top.

Christmas was fast approaching as carols belted themselves out from beneath the October calendar. Already, gift catalogues were being distributed around the staff room. Any surplus copies were scribbled on, or folded into paper planes in the common room. On seeing the order forms, Shaun and I completed them with false names and addresses.

Sebastian, a chestnut-haired fourteen-year-old, sat colouring in pictures. After filling in the last page of *The Junior Bumper Fun Book* with felt tip, he looked for any white spaces. Determined to finish his task, he quickly obliterated these with colour. Some pages near-disintegrated with ink. On closing the book, he used it as a rest for a large, self-drawn, picture of The Mister Men Meeting Mister Ben at the Train Station. Naturally, the train-driver had a moustache and glasses.

"I like moustaches," said Sebastian, raising his head.

"I can see," remarked Derek Dell.

"I like glasses."

"I can see."

"Men wear glasses. Men have moustaches."

"So do some women," I whispered to Shaun.

"I like men who have moustaches. I like men who wear glasses," said Sebastian. "When I grow up I want to be a man. A train-driving man, with a moustache and glasses."

His ambitions varied from day to day, fluctuating from train-driver to bus-driver, from taxi-driver to postman, from spaceman to policeman, but always back to the paramount train-driver. All ambitions involved the Groucho Marx combination.

"What're you drawing now?" I asked, peering towards Sebastian over the shoulder of Shaun.

"I'm drawing a postman. I'm drawing a postman like Postman Pat. He has a letter in his hand."

"Who's the letter for?"

"The postman's dad."

"I'm drawing Captain Scarlet!" added Peter. Sidling up to Sebastian's ear, he hollered: "THIS IS THE VOICE OF THE MYSTERONS!"

Grabbing a hold of the frustrated artist, Peter continued his rendition. Wrapping his arm firmly around Sebastian's shoulder, he rescued him from the aforementioned Mysterons.

"Too loud, Peter," complained Sebastian politely.

"THIS IS THE VOICE OF THE MYSTERONS!"

"Peter, please quiet."

"Run, run! They're coming!"

"Where from?" asked Sebastian, unconvinced.

"Outer space," whispered Peter. "Outer space."

"Outer space?"

"Yes! OUTER SPACE! Run, RUN! They're coming!" he warned, before bellowing: "LOST IN SPAAAACE!"

Rising to his feet, Peter Samson furiously hummed the theme tune into his coat toggles. Spreading out his wings like a space-shuttle, he ran into orbit around the common room. Knocking over a pot of pens, he reached the stars.

"Peter, pick them up!" ordered Derek Dell, losing some of his superficial cheeriness.

"Errrrr! Errrr!" hummed Peter. "Errrrrr! SPAAACE!"

"Peter, pick up the pens, please."

"Errrrr! Errrrrrrrr! LOST IN SPACE! Der! Der! Der!"

"Peter…"

"NO!"

"Peter, pick them up now! There'll be no Ribena or T.V. if you don't!"

Mumbling to himself, he issued a reluctant "Okay, oh-kay".

"Peter's been bad," said Sebastian, raising his eyes from beneath his thick, chestnut thatch.

"Peter's always bad!" chorused Simon from across the room. "That Sammo! 'E's always bad! A bad lad. Peter Samson's a bad lad!"

Winking, Simon threw several extra pens in Peter's direction as Derek Dell left the room for a coffee.

"Bad Peter Samson! No T.V. or Ribena! 'E's a bad lad! A silly old lallall! Nah, not like our Shaun! Shaun's not a lallall, 'e's bonny! A bonny lad is our Shaun. That'll teach ya!" More pens flew in Peter's direction.

In the language of Simon, a *lallall* was a silly or foolish person. The accolade of being *bonny*, or one of his *sexy best mates*, was a high one.

Smiling heartily, Simon flicked open the tape deck.

"Got any of your Duran Duran or Kylie?" asked the unofficial D.J.

"Yeah. Thanks, Simon. You've got cool taste in music."

"I love yusic!"

Pressing the play button, he stood before the crowd. An adored figure, he turned up the volume.

"Listen to the yusic, gang!" he cried, scrabbling for more rectangular fragments of his true love.

"No music!" snapped Peter from his puzzle. "T.V.!"

"Watch telly later, lallall Sammo," ordered Simon from his musical stronghold. "Me an' Shaun love yusic. Get up and dance!"

Jovially, Simon began hurling himself around the room, a chair and a picture frame getting in his way. A book flew from the mantelpiece, landing on Shaun's head. Glancing at its title, the unamused Shaun handed it to Elena who tossed it into the wastepaper bin. Reaching over, Sebastian rescued it. The book was *Jasper and Casper Learn about Health and Safety*.

As Sebastian began to read aloud, Simon interrupted him, urging his friend to dance. A small group had assembled on the "dance floor". Amongst them, Ritchie screeched like Concorde hitting the sonic boom. Walking towards the crowd, Jonathan gave me his hand. Around me were many boy–girl couples. Derek Dell, returning to his seat, nodded with quaint satisfaction.

"Errrr! Errrr!" Peter Samson decided to join the mini-disco.

Tightly squeezing the wrist of Sebastian, he dragged his partner up from the carpet. Uprooted, Sebastian mumbled a little before giving in. Swaying in time to the music, the couple looked content, save for a downcast look on Sebastian's face.

Rising from his *comfy chair* beside the radiator, Derek Dell strode through the dancing sea. Separating the twosome, he partnered Sebastian with Calista whilst Peter chose to dance alone.

"Why can't they dance together, Derek?" I asked the starch of his shirt.

"Because it's inappropriate," he nodded sternly.

"How come?"

"Because it's inappropriate."

Sighing, I returned to the music, losing my rhythm slightly. Jonathan was not the inventive type, choosing merely to sway from one foot to the other, hands locked permanently around my wrists.

"How do you dance on your own, Jonny?"

No reply.

"Can you dance with your arms?"

My wrists remained captive. Wrenching them free, I saw Jonathan move on to another partner: female, of course. He knew the rules. He'd been in the care of the company since kindergarten.

Enjoying my new single status, I raised my arms to the beat, inventing a few moves of my own. Sidling past the stereo, I noticed Elena dancing unhappily with Oliver Green, a quiet, blond boy in a Flintstones T-shirt. Long, dark hair covering her face, eyes downturned, she looked jaded, forlorn. That, I had noticed, was her usual expression. Oliver, like Jonathan, was a foot-swayer. Elena released herself from his grasp.

Courteously pairing the now lonesome Oliver with Sally, I grasped Elena's hands in partnership. Raising her head, she scratched a chunk of skin from my palm. Wincing, I swore beneath my breath. Luckily, nobody heard. Laughing, she dug in her nails.

"Bugger!"

"Heeee-heeeeee!" she giggled. "Whaddayacalllmee-Elena! Elena!"

Swinging her arms along with mine, we had a little routine going.

Five minutes had passed. Derek Dell still sat with his coffee. Marking down a rota, he barely raised his head.

"What activities am I down for?" I called from across the floor.

"Laundry, then prepare supper," he replied, head to the paper.

"But I haven't been out of the building for a week, and Simon's been out three nights running."

"That's 'cos Simon's in the Quality Street Gang!" smiled Derek. "Aren't you, Simon?"

Beaming his handsome smile, Simon hugged Derek's shoulder. "Quality Street Gang!"

"And after break, Simon, it's off to the chippy!"

"Yeah! Good old bonny Uncle Derek! Loads o' chips! Tata sauce!"

GOOD OLD
UNCLE
DEREK!

"Can I have some chips?" I asked. Dancing had given me an appetite.

"Yes," said Uncle Derek. "There's chips for all of us. That is, once you've helped prepare the bread, teas, coffees and Horlicks for the supper. Once you and all the other lasses have buttered the breads, there'll be a fine feast!"

His joviality and favoured benevolence stung me. One way for Simon, one way for the *lasses*.

Suddenly, I wanted chocolate as well as chips. Earlier, I had wanted to go to the shop for a Milky Way and some Maltesers for my break. I had been disallowed from doing so.

"None of the other young people are allowed to go shopping by themselves," Derek had said with strict disdain.

"I know, I know. But, look! I'm only buying chocolate. It's not like I'm buying arms."

"I'm sorry," Uncle Derek had replied without a note of apology. "It's considered a risk for residents to leave the building by themselves."

Unsatisfied, I had made do with a papery banana and a weak glass of orange juice.

"Fruit's better for you," Eva had reassured me. "You want to watch your figure, don't you?"

Earlier, before the long holiday spent in my bedroom, before I had been expelled from school, Dad had remarked that I looked a little "heavy". I had worried slightly, but thought nothing of it. However, the encroaching fear of being fat and the way my stomach protruded against my jeans caused me some distress.

Chips seemed a welcome reward for the toils that lay in store. An apple and some pinky Ribena seemed uninspiring. If I had to work, I would work for chips.

"Right!" called Uncle Derek, tapping his watch. "Group one – go down to the domestic science room!"

Domestic Science was merely an elaboration of the word *cookery*. Cheese straws and scones were the usual favourite. Often, large quantities of raisins or grated cheese would find themselves slowly picked away by eager fingers. As a *more able* resident, I was bestowed with the agony of watching others served first. This taxed my appetite terribly. Once my turn came, if there was anything left on the tray, I would be scolded for wolfing my food.

Richie and Sally annoyed me at table. Instead of keeping their food inside their mouths, they would distribute it around the entire lower jaw, cheeks swollen like those of squirrels tucking into a feast of acorns. Nobody told them off. They knew no better.

The butter made my fingers sticky and the bread was too springy to slice. I never ate butter myself. I preferred margarine. Anything I did not like, I said I was allergic to.

As a sliver of greasy yellow fell from the knife to my hand, I groaned loudly, rushing over to the sink.

"What's the matter now?" asked Marie.

"Urgh! Eeeurgh!" I grimaced. "It's the BUTTER! Eeeurgh! It's burning my skin!"

"No it's not," she said, matter-of-factly. Marie was always matter-of-fact. "Last time, you were allergic to coffee."

"And I still am. It makes my throat swell up and go all acidic."

"You can drink water instead, or milk."

"Water and milk are okay, if boring. It's just tea, coffee and gravy. And lamb. I'm allergic to lamb too. You know the horrible white bits? Those fatty, greasy bits? They go all solid when the meat gets cold. I'm allergic to that. It makes me vomit then gives me chronic heartburn."

Nodding her head, Marie assisted Elena with the dishes.

Marie, the great Matter-of-Factly one, had a small, friendly heart-shaped face. Her brown eyes, almost childlike, glimmered with mischief and dreams. When she smiled, the responsibilities of her twenty-three years were gone.

As a teenager, she had been the star striker in a football team. Later, in her early twenties, she had travelled around Europe and Asia, trekking to Kathmandu.

"Can I have my bread with margarine, please? Oh, and a glass of water 'cos my throat's all dry?" I yearned.

"Okay, okay, I'll let you off this time," she smiled.

I liked it when she let me off.

"Do you like the film *The Lost Boys*?"

"Yeah. It's one of my faves." She had good taste.

An avid fan of cinema, she offered me a copy of the soundtrack. Overjoyed, I revealed my adoration of Corey Feldman.

"Corey Haim's nicer," she disagreed with me.

"What about Jason Patric or that vampire with the long, black hair who gets 'death by stereo'?"

"They're pretty gorgeous, but not as gorgeous as my Damon."

Marie was soon to be married to Damon, a young classroom assistant. Tall, dark and uncharacteristically handsome, he was a great admirer of film, music and literature, but sadly not football. Sometimes he would start the day with a little-known quote from Oscar Wilde. On other days, he would recite lyrics from Pink Floyd.

I was a member of the elite group invited to Damon and Marie's wedding.

"You know something?" suggested Marie. "You were right when you said Richie looked like Fred Savage."

"Yeah. Good-looking lad."

"The other day," she began, "Richie ran away from the classroom when Damon was teaching him signs. We spent all day looking for him in the building. Murray, the cook, found him in the cupboard stealing raw Brussels sprouts and marmite. He'd already eaten six Oxo cubes."

Pausing, she dried the saucers on a towel.

"Yesterday," she continued, "he'd been good all day. He'd done all his puzzles brilliant, finished off all his dots and done his signs perfect, so I let him have an Oxo cube as a reward."

"Were you supposed to?"

"Not really," she said with a proud note of rebellion. "But *I* thought it would be appropriate. Derek told me off, but Richie loves Oxo cubes. Why not give them to him as a reward? It stops him needing to steal them."

Elena buttered bread whilst I margarined. Calista's hair had fallen from its clip.

There was a knock at the door.

"Chips are ready!" called Simon.

"Coming!" called Marie.

Lifting the tray, I followed Marie with the coffee. In her pocket she kept an Oxo cube for Richie.

— SEVEN —

SEATED UPON A plastic chair, Calista was Rapunzel. Behind her stood the Amazon Twins, Sybil Alderson and Steff Brown. Both of them scraping five-foot-eleven and possessing of tightly ringleted brown hair, they fought, legginged and trainered, for dominance over Calista's tresses. Freshly permed and freshly made-up, Calista was daubed in hues of Paris Pink and Calypso Rose. Each bitten nail was remedied with polish and each tiny flaw in her skin was concealed with powder and rouge. What was *rouge*?

Each chemical curl was wound intricately around the tongs. Her eyes were brought alive with mascara, lashes arching gracefully towards her eyebrows.

"When's it my turn?"

"Wait until it IS your turn, Jessica! You're too impatient!"

An Amazon Twin handed me the Immac.

"Go to the bathroom and put this on your legs. Marie might give you a hand."

"Does it sting?"

"No. It just makes your legs bald."

After Immac-ing, I felt better. With my monkey legs gone, I was proud to be bald.

"You'll be flashing them to all the lads now."

Standing in the corner in my dressing-gown, I watched Sabrina rock.

"Sabrina! Stop moving!" snapped Steff. "I'm trying to put your hair up. Don't pick your lips!"

Rising from the lipstick, Sabrina danced to non-existent music. Flailing her arms, high above her head, she danced into a frenzy. Sabrina was not slim. Her large breasts bounced as her knees shot higher.

"Remember, Sabrina," warned Sybil, "it's fruit for pudding, not lemon pie!"

"No pudding, only fruit," repeated Sabrina from habit.

"That's right. Fruit makes you nice and slim."

"Five-foot-five and nine-and-a-half stone," whispered Steff to Sybil. "Better keep an eye on her at table."

Calista was the same height as Sabrina, but slimmer. She was eight stone three.

"How heavy are you?" I asked Sybil, absent-mindedly.

"None of your business," she replied.

I was okay, for now. I could still have the odd pudding.

"Can I have *my* hair done?" I asked Sybil.

"Why don't you try doing it yourself for a change?"

For a change? I always did my hair myself. Every day, I would tease it to curl under, but every day it would deliberately curl *out*.

"Bugger!"

I had never applied make-up in my life, save for when my sisters and I had done ourselves up as Thundercats for fun. Sucking in my cheeks, I tried to apply the rouge from the shared make-up box. All the girls shared a large box of cosmetics, each item donated by staff who believed in the blossoming of young beauty.

Amongst the quartets of azure-blue eye-shadow and cracked compacts of mandarin face powder, I picked up a greasy red lipstick. It was red. *Rouge* was French for red, I had learned earlier in lessons.

Reluctantly, Calista let me look in the mirror she was hoarding before flashing a smile into it herself.

Marie had let me borrow a navy-blue dress suit for the wedding, as I had no money. Calista had earlier been on a spending spree.

"Oh, very nice!" remarked Steff, holding up Calista's new jacket. "It will really match that new skirt that Calista's wearing, won't it?"

"Oh yes!" added Sybil. "The pink will really match her cheeks."

Knowingly, the subject of their conversation nodded her head.

"Calista's curly hair," she sparked with white teeth. "Calista's got lovely long, curly golden hair and blue eyes with lovely long eyelashes."

Yesterday, Calista had left a piece of writing on the desk. It had repeated those familiar lines several times.

"Scrunch! Scrunch!" continued Calista. "Calista's curly hair goes *scrunch* under the curling tongs! Curling tongs! Curling tongs. Curly hair. Curly hair for Calista."

Upstairs, I changed for the wedding. Marie had been nervous all week, her voice rising and falling with excitement.

"I just hope Damon remembers to get out of bed on the big day!" she had laughed over tea. "I know one person, apart from myself, who'll be drunk the night before."

"Gettin' married in a big church!" Simon had added. "Aye, I'd like to dance at yer weddin'!"

Sitting down on the pew, I straightened my hair in the breeze. Calista strained her eyes down, past the pages of the hymn book, towards the ends of her curls. As the singing began I failed to recognise either the tune or the words, but mimed with vigour. Sebastian sat beside me, commenting on how much he liked Damon's suit.

As the march began to play, I saw the matter-of-factly angelic Marie tread slowly down the aisle in her gown. Gliding along in traditional white, I imagined her feet floating, hovering beneath the long, ivory train. Obedient bridesmaids accompanied her towards the altar.

Marie getting married?

Joining the tall, dark and genuinely handsome Damon, clean-shaven for once, the couple took their vows. Many hankies were waved and confetti fell like the dandruff of angels.

Photographs were taken in the wind. Damon's top hat proved most popular among the younger guests. Bride, groom and company posed for the photographer. The usual mistakes were obliterated with laughter as Sebastian placed the hat over his grinning head.

– EIGHT –

"I'M LATE! I'M late!"

"Shaun Rogers! Go back and do it again properly."

Reluctantly, the White Rabbit burrowed back into the curtains.

"This time do it with a little more emotion!" yelled the Queen of Hearts, waving her sceptre with fury.

Springing from behind his velvet warren, the rabbit bounded, hesitantly, across the platform. Tapping his watch with sullen grace, he hopped morosely around the stage in an off-set circle.

Giving a quietly stifled, then disconcertingly manic, burst of laughter, the Mad Hatter wrung his silver-studded cuffs with amusement. Clicking his wrists and cracking his knuckles, he applauded the unwilling Rabbit for his perseverance.

"Neil Proshka!" snapped the Queen. "Don't encourage him!"

"I'm late," murmured the White Rabbit. "I'm er...late." Checking his script for the next line, he produced a diluted "The Queen shall have my head for this."

"Shaun!" Her Highness was becoming impatient. "Read the lines with some vigour!"

"The QUEEEEEN shall have my HEAD for THIS!" he called, giving his all.

"So wooden he creaks," nudged Damon to Vince.

Turning around in his plastic director's chair, Vince studied the entire hall, viewing the remnants of a sorry cast. Joined by young people of primary and secondary ages from other branches of the Autistic Society, the actors ran riot, squabbling over sandwiches and Diet Coke rather than starring roles. Simon, a fitting Knave, was refusing to make an appearance, choosing instead to clamber up and down a loose ladder backstage. Dropping props onto the head of Sebastian, a lethargic March Hare, he let out a loud piping for every hit. Elena, the unwitting Dormouse, gave a small whimper from inside the cardboard teapot. Peter had placed a box upon his head, choosing to be an astronaut rather than a Wonderland juror.

Redwall Community Centre was a large, draughty building. Shaun likened it to a semi-deserted bingo hall. Inside the belly of its hollow vastness, temperatures could reach those colder than outside. Huddled up inside his coat, Vince could only watch as his precious creation mutated into a carnival of chaos.

"Come up 'ere, Vince!" called Simon, cliffhanging over the rafters. "It's good fun. You can see everybody acting like lallalls from up 'ere!"

"I'd rather you came down," suggested Vince with concern.

"You'd rather Peter Samson came down," giggled the stage-monkey.

"Peter Samson is sat there in the corner with a box on his head," stated Vince. "Simon Hirst does not have a stuntman's licence, so can he please come down."

"In a min. Come on down! THE PRICE IS RIGHT!"

Leaning over, Damon cast his face in an expression of deep despair: "Oh! The perils of being an ac-tor!"

Behind him sat a double row of primary-age children dressed as various flowers and small animals. As a badger pulled his hair, he winced slightly, before being poked in the shoulder by a water rat.

"Neil!" snapped Damon, catching sight of the Mad Hatter with a pen between his teeth. "Will you stop twiddling? You're supposed to be an actor, for Chrissakes!"

He had lost his usual, if saintly, patience.

Twiddling was considered not merely an irritation, but a civil offence. Without realising it, I also had been twiddling: with a rolled up script.

"Where's our Alice?" asked Damon to Vince.

"That's a point."

Finding an old, shredded newspaper under his seat, Neil picked up his pen, scrawling down the legend: "ALICE? WHERE THE FUCK IS ALICE?"

Shaun laughed, but even his laughs came out as grumbles. His ears were stinging from Sellotape wounds.

I was not Alice. I was more like a saucy French waitress. My short, frilly blue dress was pure 'Allo 'Allo meets the Carry On series. Much to Neil's amusement, my white bib, supposedly some sort of proper Victorian attire, merely pushed the frills upwards and outwards, making me look as though I had wind up my skirt.

"Curiouser and curiouser," I read woodenly.

"A little more va-va-voom!" called Damon. "At least you've got the words right."

"Curiouser and curiouser. I'm sure I saw a white rabbit..."

Shaun made his entrance.

"Errr...Late," he stammered nervously, "I'm l-late. I'm late! Ffffor a very important date."

"Hello, Mister White Rabbit," I winced.

"Nnno t-time to say...hello...goodbye," read Shaun in slow motion. "Hang on!" he noted suddenly. "Isn't Hello Goodbye a song by the Beatles?"

Voices groaned in unison as he re-took his cue.

"Jeremy Beatles!" howled the hysterical Neil. He was allowed to laugh. He was, after all, the Mad Hatter.

"I'm late, I'm late, I'm late," sighed Shaun, dragging his paws across the floorboards.

"Again, Shaun!" called the Queen of Hearts.

"I'm late."

"You're always late!" cried the observant Damon. "Late for all your cues."

"Very droll," groaned Vince.

"Alright, Shaun," shouted Damon, releasing the Rabbit from his perpetual lateness. "You can have a rest now."

"What next?" asked Vince, already knowing, and dreading, the truth.

"*The Swimming Song*," despaired Damon, mopping his brow theatrically.

The song in question played a key role in the Mock Turtle's major scene. Some of the youngest children, dressed as various crabs, winkles, tuna fish, and even a seahorse, assembled themselves into a circle, joined at the wrists. Glued into this dance formation by similarly jaded members of staff, they rotated jerkily, skipping clumsily around a rather surly looking Mock Turtle.

"I'm supposed to be a teenager!" sobbed the beleaguered Turtle, wringing a hankie. "Supposed to be a Teenage Mock Hero Turtle!"

Simon giggled, pointing to the T-shirt under his Knave's jacket.

"But I'm forty! *Forty*!" sobbed the poor Mock Turtle, lapsing gracelessly onto his rock.

"Never mind," consoled the little seahorse. "It's your birthday. Let's celebrate by singing *The Swimming Song*."

"That sounds like a good idea."

"A one, two, three, FOUR!"

Slowly, the sea-circle swung into motion.

"LOST IN SPAAAACE!" boomed Peter from behind the curtain.

"Sssssh."

The song began.

"La la la la la la-laaah. La la la la la la-laaah! La la la lallall la laaah!"

Thud, turn, skip around.

"Keep on swimming, keep on swimming, keep on swimming along!"

Miming a swimming motion, I followed the tide. The children, desperately trying to free themselves of their hold, struggled against the undertow.

"Clap your fins and stamp your tail! Flap your flippers to the beat!"

A few flapped their flippers, save for the majority who preferred to twiddle.

The crab broke free with his pincers. Furiously, he threw his head against the floor. Beating his ribs with a bandaged hand, he wept with anxiety.

"Gareth's fallen over," alerted Stacey.

"I'll take him to sit on the blanket," offered Roisin.

Roisin, a look of concern in her large, hazel eyes, ran over in black to his aid. Calming him away from the height of the stage, she guided him over the chair tops to his place of safety. Seating herself beside his trembling form, she handed him his twiddle, a toy piano. Sadly, there were no batteries and no notes sprang from the keys. In the absence of its music, Gareth began to sing, high-pitched choirboy voice forming no words, only pure, melodic sound. On finishing his song, he banged his head with his fist.

"Try the duvet," urged Stacey.

"The duvet doesn't work with Gareth," stated Roisin. "I'll try a hold."

Firmly, yet trying her best to be gentle, Roisin held his fists behind his back to prevent further damage.

Gareth eminated a series of notes that spelt out: "No banging."

"No banging. That's right, Gareth."

Suddenly, a wide grin spread out across Gareth's face. Releasing his fist, he continued to bang, twisting his other, now free, hand inside his belt. He laughed as his wrist turned purple.

"Gareth," scolded Roisin, removing his piano, "stop banging and you'll get your piano back."

"Pi-a-no," he sang, eyes following the object of desire.

"Piano. That's right."

Folding his arms tightly, he pleaded innocence.

"Piano. There you go, Gareth."

It was his.

Whooping with delight, Gareth took flight across the chairs with the magical instrument. Shrieking from the top of the scale, he hollered out an octave of joy.

"Oooh-woooh! Oooh-woooh!"

"Ah! Sympathy for the Devil," smiled a knowing Damon.

As *The Swimming Song* ended, the cast left the stage for a break. Simon, having disappeared, was now the topic of concern. Shaun too had vanished.

Wandering over towards the curtain, I knew their whereabouts. Simon, hanging one-armed from the ladder, was picking up various hats from the props department and placing them, in turn, in unusual angles upon his head. Settling on a gold-sprayed crown, he elected himself king. Shaun had found a decaying trunk of old books, many of them missing vital pages. Fumbling deeper, he found an archaic copy of *The Saint: A Novel Based on the Popular Television Series*. A look of intense satisfaction glowed from his face as he placed the treasure in his bag. He had already taken a spare copy of H. Rider Haggard's *She* for the picture of Ursula Andress on the jacket. A few detective novels fell beneath his feet. One of the badly drawn private eyes resembled Derek Dell.

"A-ha! It's our Uncle Derek!" chuckled Simon in his kingly crown.

"You know what climbing these ladders reminds me of?" asked Shaun to his regal friend. "The film *Confessions of a Window Cleaner*, starring Robin Asquith. There's this scene where he's climbing up this ladder to this blonde's house and they both get it on, covered in foam."

"Foam!" laughed Simon, wrapping a stray strand of tinsel around his shoulders.

"And in *Confessions of a Pop Performer*, also starring Robin Asquith, there's a band called Kipper…"

"Kipper!" hooted Simon, hurling himself onto a box of decorations.

"And the drummer in Kipper, played by Robin Asquith, loses his clothes backstage after shagging a groupie and has to go up on stage through an air-shaft."

"Up the shaft!"

"And when he can't find his clothes, he picks up a bundle. It's a dress!"

"Ha! A dress! Uncle Derek in a dress!" Simon rejoiced. "Ha! Old Uncle Derek on stage in a kipper dress!"

"And he gets up behind his drum-kit in a dress and gets his foot stuck in the curtain rope."

"Ha! Uncle Derek in a kipper dress on stage!"

"And then he gets hoisted up into the air."

"Old Uncle Derek flying up into t' air in a kipper dress like a great big fairy godmother! Ha for a laugh!"

"Can *you* see it?" Shaun asked me.

I could already picture the scene. Smiling at its absurdity, I broke out in a laugh.

"He'd be singing *Fairy Cross The Mersey!*" added Shaun on a roll.

"Your fantasies are both weird and cool," I said, recalling the surreal nature of the conversation.

"Have you got a fantasy?" asked Shaun.

"Yeah," I grinned wildly. "We're on stage performing the play, and then suddenly Duran Duran fly through in a jumbo jet. Simon Le Bon throws Stacey through the window. She lands in a pond, like the one in the *Wild Boys* video. Then John Taylor comes onto the scene, like the great hero he is, and liberates us all."

"Is Robin Asquith in this fantasy?"

I still had no idea who Robin Asquith was, other than that he was an actor of sorts.

"Yeah," I continued. "While John Taylor is liberating us, Robin Asquith puts on the magic dress, turns, at flashpoint, metamorphosing into Uncle Derek before gaining the power of flight. After using this newly found power to propel himself to the ceiling, he suddenly falls down as the earth opens up. In the crevasse is…"

"A load of purple milkshake and a purple turtle!" added the inspirational Simon.

"So Uncle Derek, in his dress, falls headlong into the purple milkshake before being eaten alive by the purple turtle."

"He floats down, doesn't he," suggested Shaun. "He floats down like the Toffee Crisp wrapper in that advert. The tune, dum-de-dum -dum, dum-de-dum-dum, is playing in the background. That tune is actually called *Whispering Grass* by the way. I've got it on vinyl. Anyway, as he's floating down from the ceiling, his skirt opens up like a parachute. As he floats, he looks down and begins to scream the lyrics to *Fairy Cross The Mersey*, before being swallowed up by the purple turtle."

"The turtle licks his lips," added Simon.

"And what are me and John Taylor doing?" I asked Shaun, hungrily.

"You're backstage, having mad sex in the foam."

The thought was exciting, yet it made me wince slightly. John Taylor had dignity! Sex rarely crossed my mind. Kissing John Taylor seemed romantic and fun, but I had never considered the Dirty Deed until now. Closing my eyes without blushing, I imagined.

"Ah, look," said Shaun, picking up another private detective tome. "It's Vince!"

"Vince in an old anorak, like what Uncle Derek wears!" giggled Simon, his voice almost girlish.

Sex with John Taylor? What *was* sex like? What would sex with John Taylor be like?

Suddenly, the real Vince made an appearance. He had homed in on our alternative world of yellowed pages and paper crowns. Quickly, the Saint, Ursula Andress and the private eye doppelgangers hid themselves back inside the trunk.

"I hope you lot aren't endangering yourselves," he asked with concern. "After all, the White Rabbit is a much-coveted role."

Silently, Shaun left his hollow. Simon, placing a pirate's hat on his head, skipped over to welcome Vince into our hideaway. Occasionally looking up from a bedraggled Top of the Pops annual, I allowed the visitor to take a seat beside me on the box.

Vince cast his eye over us suspiciously.

"We were method acting," I told him. "We came back here to make Wonderland seem more real. See, this *is* Wonderland. Oh, and we've been reading literature. It's very educational."

"Good book, this!" cackled Simon, flinging a tattered murder mystery at Shaun.

"I actually recommend this one," said Shaun, picking up a book at random.

It was a long-winded courtroom saga with a did-he-didn't-he theme concerning a would-be presidential assassin. Shaun already had his eyes glued to the back cover.

"I see that you are all avid readers," said the dry Vince. "How about reading your scripts for once? You might just remember your lines."

I hung my head in shame, along with my companions.

"Isn't it time you came out with the rest of us and stopped all this nonsense?" hollered Damon from behind the curtain.

"Nonsense," I sighed before yelling: "But we have to experience real nonsense before acting out all the pretend nonsense in the play."

"Logic, logic," sighed Damon in defeat.

"Simon! Get down from the rafters!" called Vince. "You could get hurt!"

"But he's the Knave of Hearts," I explained. "He's only turning his role into reality. He's method acting."

"Come on stage, gang," urged Vince. "Let's rock 'n' roll."

"Do I have to sing *Cats and Rabbits*?" I protested.

"Yes."

"But that's not even rock 'n' roll."

"Give it another try."

"I can't bloody sing. I'm useless!"

"Of course you can," flourished Damon. "You're our star!"

Flattery got him nowhere.

"I'm a crap singer, mind you," I paused. "Can I have a Kit-Kat if I sing slightly less than crap?"

"We'll see."

Reluctantly, we trod the boards. Roisin had to suffer in the guise of a large brown rabbit. Oliver Green was content to play an oversized kitten.

"Real nonsense," I murmured.

– NINE –

"KEEP ON SWIMMING, keep on swimming, keep on swimming aaaa-looong!"

After packing our bags, we hurriedly took our seats in the bus: a large, blue dilapidated Ford Transit. Those who sat near the back door were in danger of a fall out. A fickle lock had been placed there to combat this problem, but to little avail. More often than not, the padlock found its way into Simon's pocket. Inside, the synthetic grey seats were torn open in places, allowing the nylon stuffing to spill out. Stains from Ribena and other substances patterned the floor.

Fortunately, due to my lack of a sense of smell, I was relieved of the fragrance that usually arose after a call of "Marty's wet!". However, my phobia of germs gave me a phantom nasal power. I was ever alert to such paranoia.

Marty was seated behind Richie and me. Although the cause of the stench was invisible to me, I could still make out each speck, watch each bacterial form multiply before my eyes. A hand reached up to touch my shoulder. The hand belonged to Marty.

"Aaargh! Eva! Can I change my jumper, please?"

"No!" she snapped like a bitter biscuit.

"But Marty touched me and he's wet."

"He only touched you."

"But Marty puts his hands down his pants."

"You can cope with it."

"But I have germs on my shoulder."

"Stop being so obsessional!" harped the angry Eva. "Any more of this talk and you won't go swimming."

Silently, I tried to live with the colony of bacteria on my shoulder. The patch of skin beneath my jumper began to itch uncontrollably. I could feel them climbing up my neck and onto my face. Soon I would be nothing more than a living, breathing, writhing mass of germs. I was contaminated.

Checking my hands, I noticed the fingertips were slightly dusty from touching the window. Panic struck me. Not only was the entire upper half of my body infected, my hands had become cesspools. I could not touch anyone or anything throughout the journey. Instead I would have to keep my hands to myself in order to avoid spreading the disease. If I did touch anyone, I would surely start a plague. The germs would reign supreme!

Sitting like a leper, I pulled on my gloves. They would need to be washed and disinfected once I removed them. My hair would also need washing, as I imagined Marty, the plague-starter, had touched that also.

Edging away from Richie, I isolated myself.

"Stop flinching! The chlorine will remove the germs."

I was allergic to chlorine. It stung my eyes and made my hair tatty. No amount of soap and shampoo could ever remove chlorine from my body. I could scrub away my skin and still the chlorine would be present in my flesh. Perhaps chlorine, like germs, penetrated right to the bone, straight into the marrow, where it would stay, irremovable, for ever.

Inside my body, I imagined an everlasting battle between the opposing evils of chlorine and bacteria.

Eva started up the engine. Rattling with frost, it roared into action and the bus left the yard. As the windows steamed up, I thought of all the horrors that blossomed within congealed breath. Simon wrote the name of a football team across the back pane. I feared for his finger.

Uncle Derek handed Eva a tape. Before it even slotted itself into the cassette-deck, I knew the journey would become, yet more, unbearable.

It was a Christmas tape. Nat King Cole crooned on side one. On the second side warbled Paul McCartney and festive friends. I had been disallowed my Duran Duran privilege due to an incident over table.

The ban arose from my refusal to eat gravy. Brown and sticky, like quagmire slurry, it turned my stomach just to look at it. Holding my head as though concealing an allergy-ridden face, I had been sent away from the table. My chair had been moved away from my plate, allowing me to hunger for my roast potatoes whilst watching the others feast. On my return, my food had grown cold before being coated, by incredibly zealous staff, in tepid gravy. The food was inedible. On refusing to eat the gravy-strewn remnants that had once been food, I had to suffer fruit instead of pudding.

If I was lucky, I would still be allowed supper.

Constance Hill Hospital rose above the leafless bushes ahead. A large concrete box, it resembled a space-colony I had seen in one of Peter's videos. Remembering that the video had been *Logan's Run*, I predicted that Peter, himself, would try like Michael York to be a runner from that building.

Eva caught him mid-step and gave him a caution.

Walking down the long, white corridor, strewn with the drawings of sick children and patients' relatives, I watched as wheelchairs rolled past. Inside, I felt ashamed. I did not appear or even act disabled. What right did I have to swim in this hospital pool when others had *real* disabilities?

Elderly patients exchanged yarns with the nurses. I wished I could have stayed and joined the conversation. Instead, despite my curiosity, I was ushered towards the changing rooms.

To my dismay, the changing room only had one shower! Solitary and near-inoperable, it stood behind a slightly derailed plastic curtain. The others would, inevitably, borrow my shampoo without asking. Normally, I would be willing to share it, but Wendy Shire was known for using a whole bottle.

Wendy, a small, compact brunette, was newer to Easton House than myself. Glowing with pride, today she had awoken to a dry bed. This meant she was instantly given the privilege of swimming. Pulling her leggings down over unshaven legs, she raptured "I'm dry!" to her audience.

"Eva," I nudged, "keep Wendy away from my shampoo, please."

Normally, Wendy would shampoo her entire body.

"Can she use just a little bit?" insisted Eva.

"Alright," I agreed reluctantly. "But only a *tiny* bit."

The changing rooms were communal so I hid behind my towel before pulling myself, uneasily, into my costume.

Beside the mirror stood Calista, stroking her hair as Eva tied it up into a scrunchie. Grinning through her gritted teeth, she studied each area of her cleanly scrubbed face. Elena sat in the corner, on the bench, huddled up inside her towel. Whispering to herself loudly, she was scolded by Sybil who sent her to touch the wall.

Elena was on a *programme*. Her programme insisted that every time she touched herself on the breasts, spat, or bit her shoulder, she would be sent to touch the wall at opposite sides of the room. The logic behind this could not be explained.

"Why aren't *I* on a programme?" I asked.

"Because you're not," replied the curt Sybil.

"Why not?"

"Because you don't need one."

"Why don't I need a programme?"

"Because you're too able for a programme."

As Sybil turned away, I heard Steff whisper: "She's able alright. I don't even think she has autism."

"That's because I don't HAVE autism," I added, to put them out of their miseries.

"Then why are you here?" asked Sybil and Steff in unison.

"Because I'm unlucky."

Fair deal. They stopped the conversation.

Eventually, after many relays to the wall and back, Elena was ready. Weeping without tears, she trod through the sterilised pool into the swimming area. The water beneath her feet shone a dull, slippery yellow. Beneath her toes, the white tiles were stained brown.

Eva led the line of swimmers towards the pool. Her outstanding all-year tan glowed beneath the harsh electric lights. Those that followed her seemed like pale spectres in her wake. Tossing her stiff golden mane with leaderly pride, she was the first to dip her toes in the water. Swiftly pulling them out, she froze.

Elena gave a yelp of excitement on seeing the pool before drawing back into the safe arms of Sybil. She would wait until the floats were out. Water, by itself, was merely a big cold bath.

Suddenly, a loud flapping of bare feet echoed against the tiles. Leading the merry parade of swimming-trunked men came Simon, clad in suspiciously large and pocketed Bermuda shorts. Giving a holler, a whoop and a wave of the hand, he belly-flopped fearlessly into the pool, choosing to ignore the steps.

Shaun appeared last of all. He stood hunched and reluctant in a pair of shorts borrowed from his brother. A wry grin appeared on his ashen face as Simon's body splashed out a tidal wave.

Peter covered his face with a stray flipper. "The Man From Atlantis!" he pointed as Simon surfaced in a cloud of bubbles.

Richie took second place in the pool race, wandering towards the side of the pool, laughing and flicking water onto the sidewalk. Soaking the attendant, he let out a celebratory "Laaang-a-laaang!".

To my extreme disappointment the pool had no deep end. The shallow end spread from top to bottom without varying. Gloomily, I trod the tiled stairway, unknowingly clinging to the safety rail. As the water hit the tops of my thighs, I flinched. Walking up to waist-level, I dared lower myself to my haunches. As the water soaked over my shoulders, I shivered. Sinking no further, I preserved my precious hair from the danger of chemicals.

As I gradually became comfortable, a wave threw itself over my head and right into my sinuses. Looking around, disgruntled and in a red-eyed stupor, I spied a laughing, mocking Marie. Kicking up a storm with my legs I started a war. Simon, eager to please, fought for both sides. Soon I forgot the fact that my hair was fast deteriorating into nuclear mass of split ends and allergy-inducing chemicals, and dived under.

A mattress-sized float was launched into the choppy seas. Simon the Brave nominated himself captain of the vessel and swam towards it with determination. Sliding his belly onto the huge rectangle of foam, he paddled it over each passing pedestrian. Crushing Sebastian beneath the rudders of his feet, he sailed past, regardless of all casualties. Ignoring all caution, he sat up, gradually raising himself to a standing position. Now erect on his two strong feet, he surfed the bodies.

"C'mon, old Shaun Rogers Towel Man! Come and join me on t' big boat!"

Shaun's sullen face broke out into a fevered excitement.

"C'mon, old Shaun Rogers Towel Man! We can do stunts! Aaaa-aaaah! Watch me dive off!"

As Simon dived from the side of his vessel, Shaun seated himself at the centre, legs crossed in yogic fashion. Joining him, I straddled myself across the sinking surface, using my legs as a propeller. We had motion. As Simon returned to the crew, we sat together in a circle before rising to our feet in unison. We earned our five seconds of glory before being flung back into the shallow depths.

Giving the three of us a caution, Eva returned to the struggling Elena, the tiny limpet on the hand-rail.

Dale Widdowson clung to the stair-rail, a safety-band wrapped tightly around each muscular arm. Echoing a shrill moan, she pleaded for guidance. Although unusually small for an eighteen-year-old, standing only four foot eight, she was powerfully built, broad-shouldered and sinewy. Simon, lithe and tanned, flickered past urging her to join the flow. Terrified, she refrained. Refusing to budge, she only clenched herself tighter and tighter to the rail. Each splash of cold water seemed to burn her skin.

Marie swam over to assist. Luring Dale further into the pool, she coaxed the girl to remove her hands. For a second, she obliged. A second later, she obliterated her efforts with a loud wail. Bellowing until the pool was a nest of cacophony, she struggled in a pool of her own panic-filled ripples.

"Dale's wailin'!" yelled Simon. "Shut up, Dale! Quit the racket!"

Dale continued to wail.

Removed from the pool, she was sent to the showers, Eva following close at hand.

Earlier in the week, I had perfected my mimicry of Dale's wail and had decided to test it out in the toilets. Hiding inside the cubicle, I had begun the husky moaning. Suddenly, I felt water running down my face. Foolishly, I remembered that staff *always* threw water over Dale when she wailed in the toilets. My impersonation had been just too convincing.

"Mysterons!" called Peter, both hands be-flippered. "Mysterons loose in the pool!"

Grabbing a free hose from the sidewalk, he swung it like a lasso. Placing the flippers on his feet, he launched into a monologue: "Oh no! The squid is attacking the crew! Mysterons! Mysterons are in the water. Call Captain Scarlet! Call Thunderbird Two! Underwater. Stingray and Thunderbirds are GO! 5, 4, 3, 2, 1! LIFT OFF!"

Diving in, he gave a loud splutter.

"Silly old Peter Samson gettin' drownded again!" scolded Simon, splashing out amongst the debris.

"Help! Help!" howled Peter. "The octopus! From Mars!"

Dale's wailing echoed down the passage.

"Why do we bring her swimming, Marie?" I asked. "She looks terrified!"

"We're supposed to be getting her over her fear of water," replied Marie, clambering onto the float.

"Is it working?"

"Not really. She's petrified."

There was a small, red handprint on Marie's shoulder.

"It's from a tug-of-war," she explained. "I didn't really want to force her into the pool, she was scared, so she grabbed me."

"STINGRAY! STINGRAAAAAAY! DER-DER-DER-DER-NER-NER!"

As the attendant made the signal, we left the pool. Ahead of us lay the warmly toasted promise of chocolate krispies and hot Ribena.

Consoling ourselves with this thought, we headed towards the changing rooms.

Leaving the water, I felt every hair on my body rise with the cold. Light-headed and blurry-eyed from chlorine, I anticipated the race for the shower cubicle. Dale was still inside, her hair unflinching from its elastic band. Impatiently, I stood in second place. Every few seconds I would scour the floor with my eyes, guardian of my beloved Timotei. Eventually, I picked up the bottle, holding it to my chest as though it were ambrosia for hair.

Eagerly, I darted under the, now free, shower-head.

"Running in the changing rooms, Jessica!" snapped Sybil. "For that, you'll wait until last!"

"I'm always last," I protested angrily.

"You'll still wait until last. YOU WILL WAIT!"

"But I walked fast. I didn't run."

"Silly Jessica's gonna wait until last," said Sybil to the crowd of girls. "You can all step in the queue in front of her."

Losing my place, I dripped onto Sybil's towel. Luckily, she never noticed. Sulking, I sat, hard-done-to, on the soggy bench, casting doleful eyes at the pushers-in. A small tear of anger lumbered down my cheek, drowned beneath a lava of sweat and chlorine.

As time stretched out and my supply of Timotei diminished with each hairwash, the room grew humid. The air itself seemed a smog of bodies and chemicals. What these horrors smelt of, I would never know. Each minute in this biochemical swamp grew more unbearable.

Once I was given my turn, I was hurried out with hardly time to wash properly. There was no hair-drier. Scowling, I began to dress. Rushing with the towel, my clothes became saturated at the touch of my skin.

Damp and self-pitying, I trod my way through the windy car park. Driving home, I thought of John Taylor. His face made me smile again.

After waiting for another age in the supper queue, last again, I savoured my chocolate krispie like it was manna from the gods. In truth, there had probably been many fingers in the mixture, enlarging the bacterial content, but my hunger from that earlier humiliation forced me to eat each chocolate-coated germ. As each bite melted inside my mouth, I blinkered myself to the repulsive gnashing that surrounded me.

"French and Saunders! Saunders. Bop-sha-doody-doo!" sang a low-pitched, masculine voice.

"Why are you singing that?" I asked, perplexed.

Over my shoulder lurked a cup of coffee and Wayne. A short, stocky moustache of a man, he scoffed over my chocolate. His nickname for me was "Dawn", on other occasions, "Frenchie".

Suffering this, I turned around and asked: "Do you really think I'm fat?"

"It's just puppy fat," came Eva, back-handedly.

Puppy fat? Was I a fat dog?

Retorting, I struck out at Wayne: "You look like a FAT Freddie Mercury."

"Fat Fred!" added his sidekick, Rob.

Rob was caustically amiable. Half a foot taller than Wayne, his face was pointed and grinning above his Sex Pistols T-shirt.

"Who you callin' Fat Fred?" clowned Wayne as the two amigos created mirth.

Meanwhile, I sat worried. I was a fat dog.

"Don't worry," consoled Marie. "All that swimming will have kept you fit."

– TEN –

TOGETHER, WE DECKED the hall with boughs of plastic holly. Uncle Derek nobly brought in a tree: not a synthetic supermarket tree, but a real-life, needle dropping, splinter-hazardous tree. Unbinding it from its cellophane straitjacket, he erected it, unsuccessfully, in a small bucket filled with rocks from the garden. As the tree fell gracelessly down, Marie and Eva joined forces to keep it hovering just slightly above the carpet. Scattering itself in abundance over the heads and clothes of those beneath it, the tree seemed ungrateful for its newly earned position of importance. Wavering beside the entrance, it was soon to be adorned by the hands of many. It was to be proudly swamped with paper decorations, tiresomely and reluctantly produced by the hands of young people, and weighed down with the spendings of Derek Dell's cash donation.

Leaning hazardously, it threatened the parting of Uncle Derek's crown. Rebelliously, it broke free from the shackles of the bucket, throwing both Eva and Marie sideways. Laughing on hearing the uproar, Simon peeked his ruddy, grinning face through the doorway. Instantly, he was given the official honour of *bucket carrier*.

Swiftly fetching a larger bucket, filled heavily with stones and mud, he handed it to Uncle Derek. Resurrecting Nat King Cole on the stereo, he roused the decorators into festive cheer. Strong and skilful, Simon erected the tree. Standing back from the monument to his deed, he gave himself a round of applause.

"Bring out the baubles!"

Racing along to the supply cupboard, Marie, Eva and I took it upon ourselves as artists that this was our duty. As a shining indigo rope of tinsel caught my eye, I pulled it over my shoulders. This was *my* tinsel and *I* was going to be the one who placed it upon the tree.

Placing the box hastily down on the floor, we stood back, for less than a minute, admiring its treasures. Pulling out a stringless bauble, Marie bounced it across her knees like a football.

As Uncle Derek left for the sleep-in room to fetch the lights, we were left responsible as the wardrobe department for the naked tree.

Looping two baubles over her ears, like gigantic earrings, Marie threw a shower of gold lametta over my head. Peering through my new crowning glory, I threw a handful back. Picking up more tiny footballs to kick, Marie began the sports. Eva, kicking a pass to Simon, fell as I tackled her between the leggings. As a deflated bauble shattered against the window pane, Simon hollered "GOAL!" before running a celebratory lap around the stepladder. A penalty was taken by Marie as Eva stood, legs akimbo, as goalkeeper. Another bauble tinkled out a broken melody against the plaster. Simon threw a winner's medal around his neck in victory.

Placing a pink tinsel halo upon his head, he stood, angelic, over the box of temptations. Meanwhile, Neil Proshka and Peter Samson appeared from outside the dining room, clutching a tray of homemade mince pies. Licking his lips, Simon took two, handing one to Marie.

Thanking him, she took a huge bite, dropping crumbs onto the carpet.

"Marie! Are you dropping crumbs on the carpet?" boomed the return of Uncle Derek.

"Yes, but Eva's dropping tinsel."

"And it looks like our tree needs sorting out."

Dutifully, we returned to adorn the tree. Offering my artistic opinions, I commented on the placing of the tinsel.

"That red bit needs to go higher. Blue and green don't look good together. Put the green near the red."

Climbing up the stepladder, I raised the red tinsel closer to the zenith.

"Be careful up there, won't you?" warned Uncle Derek. "Young people aren't really supposed to climb stepladders."

"Don't worry! I *love* heights."

Earlier, I had created a tree fairy from tin foil and tissue. The face was rather Kylie-like in its proportions, but the nose was slightly too heavy. If I made a fairy too perfect, I would become envious of my own creation.

Striding over, clicking his fingers and twiddling his wrists, Neil Proshka glanced, wolfishly, up her skirt.

Neil always looked forward to Christmas. Every Yuletide holiday, he would catch a plane to Poland, celebrating with his relations. Last year he had sent back an embroidered postcard and some biscuits. His tape-box had returned filled with cheaply bought albums from Krakow. No doubt the Pet Shop Boys would reign supreme in the common room on his return.

Behind a tray of Christmas tree-shaped biscuits, Elena stammered "T-t-t-t take one!" before dropping the tray to the floor.

"Elena Kiriakos!" snapped Sybil from behind her. "Pick that tray up, then touch the wall!"

Looking up from the gingerbread debris, the terrified Elena whimpered a "No."

"You WILL touch the wall! NOW!"

"No…Elena no. Touch it! Touch it! No!"

Scrambling among pieces of trunk, branches and lametta, she picked up the tray before throwing it at a plastic Santa Claus. Falling from the wall, Santa injured his ample posterior on a pile of stones.

"No touch Elena!" Instead, she bit her hands before touching her breasts. "Not-hit-Santa!"

"Uncle Derek spent ages putting that Santa up," reminded Eva. "Now will you please touch the wall!"

After touching the wall several times she sat on the floor, exhausted, whilst Marie ordered me to fetch a vacuum cleaner.

"Ouch! Cut my finger!" she cried, holding aloft her wounded left hand. "Blood! *Bleed!*"

Sybil, noticing the injury, took it upon herself to fetch a plaster from the cupboard. The anxiously twisted face of Elena told her that a bath and bedtime were needed.

Since the first Santa Claus had appeared on the landing, since the first adverts for Christmas shopping had appeared on the television, since the first Christmas catalogues had landed in the mail, Elena had grown more disturbed and frustrated. She had only a *holiday* to look forward to, a *holiday* in a large, white, sunnily sterile building. A building full of fun, games and activities. She was going to Temperance Hill Hospital.

Elena's family adored her. When they came to visit her from home, they showered her with gifts and affection. However, she was known to display *challenging behaviour* inside the family household, thus endangering her younger siblings. Although it troubled them, their daughter would have to visit Temperance Hill on a yearly basis.

Steff brought in a pot of Horlicks. Uncle Derek rubbed his hands with glee. As Steff stepped past Neil, he swooned poetically before reaching for a handy piece of paper nearby. Scrawling an ode to his muse, he etched the words: "Skin like chocolate milkshake, bum like a ripe peach, hair like an explosion in a mattress factory."

On finishing this pen-portrait of the woman he so loved, he handed it discreetly to Shaun. Stuttering a laugh, Shaun repeated the ode to Simon, who giggled girlishly.

"Explosion in a mattress factory," hummed Shaun. "Do you reckon it was blown up by dropping bombs, or possibly ignited by a match to TNT and other explosives?"

"It was..." paused Neil thoughtfully, "an electric short circuit."

Cracking his knuckles, he rocked with exhilaration.

"Would you have sexual intercourse with Steff?" asked Shaun.

"Sexual intercourse?" he gasped. "Why sexual *of course!*"

Laughing at his pun, he rocked faster.

"Shaun! Shaun, come here a minute," called Steff. "Is it true that you had bubbles in your bath?"

"Er...I can't remember," mumbled the amnesiac Shaun. "I er...I might have."

"Then who caused that mess on the floor?"

"It were Peter Samson flickin' water again," interrupted Simon, before scolding the culprit. "Silly old lallall Peter Samson!"

"Peter, were you flicking water?" questioned Steff in disbelief.

"No-o."

"Who was flicking water then?"

"Sha-un."

"Shaun," reminded Steff, "I think you'd better go and clean it up."

"Leave our Shaun alone!" defended Simon. "'E ain't done nowt!"

As Shaun followed Steff, he caught a glimpse of her curvaceous buttocks as she climbed the stairs. Neil looked on with envy.

Chestnuts roasted on the electric grill as Nat King Cole was played again. The last decorations, small paper flowers that flew from the branches, fragile as the door blew open, were added. As the light went off, the lights went on. Everybody cheered before singing *O Christmas Tree*. Clever Neil sang *O Tannenbaum* instead.

"What is this garbage on the stereo?" mused Neil.

"Uncle Derek's Christmas tape," replied Simon.

"Ah!" exclaimed Neil with a flourish. "*Songs of Derek!*"

Neil became a human twiddle. Repeating his line of wit, he pondered its initials. Shaun, reappearing, stuttered between guffaws. Derek, busy clapping his hands to the congregation, remained oblivious.

Tearing the roof from the largest mince pie, Sebastian sat beside a box of felt-tips. Showing Derek a picture he had drawn earlier, a postman delivering letters for Santa, he walked over to show me. In truth, it looked like all the other pictures he drew: heavy black lines and relentless technicolour.

"It's a picture of a postman," he announced proudly. "A postman."

"I can see," I drawled, bored eyes watching the clock.

"He's a postman delivering letters for Santa. There is also a Santa's sack in the picture. When I grow up I want to be a postman."

"What else do you want to be when you grow up?" I asked, already knowing the answer.

"A policeman. A policeman in a hat. I would have a badge. I would have a moustache. I would wear glasses."

"What else?" I was making conversation as there was nothing else to do.

"A soldier. A soldier with a red uniform outside Buckingham Palace."

The advent calendar facing us showed a poor artistic interpretation of the Nativity.

"What else?" I asked.

"Jesus. Jesus, Jessica. Baby Jesus. Jesus loved Moses who turned the river red. I want to be Jesus when I grow up."

From the corner, Neil let out a loud splutter.

"What do you want to be, Neil?"

"A pop star!"

Grinning, he pulled from his pocket a pair of 3D glasses, a leftover from last week's film-show. Placing them atop his curly dark head, he posed for an imaginary camera. Jeanette, wandering past with a tower of empty coffee cups, winked at him.

As Simon unpeeled door no. 11 of the advent calendar, I sent my eyes searching for no. 12. Tomorrow would be my fourteenth birthday. Undoubtedly, it would be lost in the excitement for Christmas. Oh, how I cursed the baby Jesus at times!

Eva, however, had assured me of a party in my honour.

Tomorrow arrived slowly. Kept awake by my imagination, I could already see the huge hall emblazoned with flowing banners. I could see the long line of celebrity guests: John Taylor heading the queue. My cake would be iced with chocolate. It would be enormous and shaped like a record player. Smarties on the summit would spell out a huge *14*. I saw myself as the DJ, having full control of the music. There would be several Duran Duran songs, a few by Def Leppard and Bon Jovi, a couple by Kylie and Madonna. Everybody would dance, even Shaun. I would be dancing in John Taylor's embrace after the crowds had gone home. It would be *my* party.

The reality was a cleared-out dining room, each square table pushed against the wall. Carrying the vacuum cleaner from the cupboard, I lethargically tidied the floor. My hair was filthy and probably stank of whatever germs lived and bred there. There was no time for a bath during cleaning duties. Maybe I would be a birthday Cinderella? Perhaps they had all prepared a big surprise for me?

Wallowing in hopeful self-pity, I helped inflate a few balloons. Simon filled some with no problem whilst Shaun was scolded by Eva for talking instead of blowing.

"In one episode of *The Man from U.N.C.L.E.*" he began, "there were these crooks, drug smugglers, who filled some balloons with a white powder resembling LSD. Anyway, once Ilya Kuryakin caught up with them, and they were carrying out a heist in Colombia, they thought they had them…and the drugs! However, once the balloons were handed over, they were just full of helium gas, and when the president was given the evidence, he talked *liiike thiiis*!" Shaun demonstrated a gas-inflated squeak. "And the crooks escaped…in a large car, a hearse, pretending they were going to a funeral. Ilya Kuryakin crashed his moped into the back of the hearse, and there was a load of smoke…"

"Loads o' smooooke!" chorused Simon, adding sound effects to the story.

"Anyway, the car was hit and the white powder spilled out on to the road."

"Like Sherbet Dip-Dabs!" laughed Simon.

"When the crooks were caught, this man appeared from out of a helicopter…"

"Shaun!" interrupted Eva. "Just blow up the balloon and stop gassing!"

"Gas…" mused Neil. "Gas as in 'to talk', or gas as in 'gas'? Is that why some people are called *wind-bags*? Full of gas, windy gas? Wasted air? Could you light a gas fire by talking too much?"

I pictured balloons with printed messages. Perhaps the messages were talk trapped inside the balloons.

Placing out the buffet, I anticipated the arrival of the cake. It was probably too special to be brought out now. Setting up the stereo, I brought out a selection of my tapes. Neil and Simon added some of theirs. Shaun was told by Eva to keep *his* music upstairs in his bedroom.

As the clock struck six-thirty, the room filled with people. As the dance floor flooded itself, the party was born. The buffet was looked upon, through clingfilm, by eager eyes. The celebrations began. After half an hour the staff took their breaks, leaving the young people under the watchful eye of a lone Eunice. Gradually the dancers, even the fanatical Neil, who had once considered becoming a professional, filtered away to their seats. Only the lowered music warded away silence.

Uncle Derek made his return carrying my presents. The buffet was released to enliven the weary. Opening a small, rectangular package after a torrent of unwanted bath salts and shower gel, I felt a sudden joy come over me. The gift was Duran Duran's *Rio*! Delighted and disbelieving, I held John Taylor in my hands.

Placing the tape, ceremoniously, into the stereo, I gathered a crowd of eaters onto the dance floor. Sadly, food took priority over movement.

Neil, after piling his plate high, placed it in my trust as he set the floor alight with his Reeboks. Surveying the edible Wonderland before my eyes, I felt a twinge of envy towards Neil. He was a greyhound of a boy despite eating what seemed like twice his weight in saturated fat. My metabolism had settled my increasing girth at eight stone four pounds. Feeling my fat belly through my baggy jeans, I decided tomorrow to wear my dungarees, which hid it well. My arms and legs were not particularly fat, nor was my face, but my metabolism was slow and my stomach puffy. Sybil put her ample curves down to *just being a woman*. Perhaps this was true, even if she did seem more like a man at times. In the street, or at the market I visited with the staff on Saturdays, there were visibly more fat women than fat men. Perhaps fat was a female disease. Most of the males at Easton House seemed incredibly thin, save for the stocky and spreading Shaun, and plump Oliver who ate only fruit, like the girls, after his meals to keep his weight down. Most Easton females, save for Elena, who was positively emaciated due to her refusal to eat, and hyperactive Wendy, seemed either curvaceous, chubby, or just plain fat.

Sabrina suffered badly at the party. Instead of chocolate biscuits, she was handed Ryvitas with cottage cheese and pieces of fruit. Glancing longingly at the trifle that tantalised her, she bit her lips. Hungrily, she shoved a whole pear into her mouth, some of it lodging up her nose. This movement appeared bizarrely comical. Slyly, I picked two glacé cherries from the trifle, taking one for myself, giving one to Sabrina.

"We'll dance off the calories," I joked, urging her to her feet.

Flapping her arms, rocking her body furiously from side to side, Sabrina took flight. Warning her against flapping, Eva took her back to her seat. Even seated, she took to the music, each beat pulling her back and forth like a boat in a current.

Returning to the dance, I was upstaged by Neil. Flailing his arms, legs and torso with athletic precision, he was a natural. As my own efforts propelled me into second place, I re-seated myself beside Shaun. Together, we nicknamed Neil "John Revolta".

"Is my cake here yet?" I asked Eva with impatience.

"In a minute!"

Staff rushed, indiscreetly, down the corridor. There was no cake. Instead, they did their level best to decorate a plain Victoria sponge. With speed, four candles appeared on top. They had forgotten my cake! Angrily, I complained to Marie. Reassuring me of the Christmas rush, she gave her excuses. Never had my urge been stronger to hurl Santa from the wall. I cursed my luck for being a December child.

Calista, girlishly picking at the fruit cocktail, put me to shame with my slice of cake. Neil took a larger slice. He was allowed to. Calista had filled out slightly, but her immaculately painted face was still too close to perfection.

"Ca-list-a!" I cursed.

"Jealous again?" observed Eva, reading my venomous tone. "Calista can't help being born beautiful. Some of us are given the gift of being beautiful. Calista just happens to *be* beautiful."

"Prettier than me?" I spat, narrowing my eyes.

"That's not for me to say," shrugged the democratic Eva. "Some people may find Calista beautiful, while others might find you…"

"Bloody ugly!" I damned myself.

"Ugliness is only in the eye of the beholder," philosophised Marie. "Nobody's ugly unless they believe they are. Look at me!" she pointed. "I'm no fashion model, but to my Damon I'm a Greek goddess. Anyway…" she whispered, "Calista has problems much worse than yours. She has trouble with reading and spelling. And she needs to work on social skills, like conversation."

It was true that Calista had trouble forming sentences.

"She's not that perfect," continued Marie, supping her coffee. "Not perfect by a long stretch. You might not have blonde hair and blue eyes or a slim figure, but you can write well, talk well, which many of us here struggle with. And you're good at art."

"Yeah, so I can do a few crappy portraits of pop stars," I sighed. "And doodles of staff that I get in trouble for drawing."

Tired of the moralising, I thought of children's cartoons. At the end of each cartoon, the most comically misunderstood character would appear, giving the audience a touchy-feely lecture on how "looks aren't everything" or "always ask an adult to take the risks on Bonfire Night". Groaning, I returned to the buffet table.

As Calista approached and the backs of the staff were turned, I tempted her with a bowl of chocolate eclairs. Popping one casually into my mouth, I held the bowl within her reach. Gingerly taking one, then another, and then another, a smile of satisfaction came to her mouth. An even larger smile came to mine.

– ELEVEN –

"I THOUGHT YOU were going to get someone else to sing behind me!" I yelled from the wings. "I'm not doing all this bloody singing by myself!"

A shudder of fear ran down my knee-socks as I took a sly glimpse at the audience. Before the isolated stage spread a simpering sea of senior staff and smartly dressed parents. Side partings, executive jackets, polished spectacles and mahoganied coiffures all filled the murmuring atmosphere.

A sycophant clapped me on the back suddenly: "Oh, I didn't realise you were only a *young person*! I thought you were *staff*. You look so *able*."

Muddled by nerves, I wandered around in a circle of confusion. Able. I was able. I was so able that I dreamed the word in my sleep.

"I can't bloody sing! Get bloody Calista to do it! You're always saying how great she is. Why get me up here? I'm a *non-singer*!"

"Aaaaah!" blew Damon, rolling out his words in waves. "Here is the DRAMA QUEEN!"

Drama queen. I was a drama queen. I was the queen of drama, whose every hint of emotion was dubbed part of a farce. My "drama" was betraying the fact that I was able. Able people did not panic. Able people did not throw tantrums. Able people did not swear, cry or make a fuss. I was a living contradiction to this unwritten rule.

"Show starts in ten minutes."

"Ten minutes?"

"Ten minutes!"

Ten minutes, ten minutes, ten minutes.

I wanted to scream, to run, to hide, to panic, but not to sing. I could sing in my bedroom. I could sing in the garden. I could sing over the boredom of kitchen duties, but I could not sing to parents and seniors.

"Take a deep breath," advised Damon, himself slightly disgruntled.

"Can I not have a loud scream instead?"

"Count to ten."

"One…two…three," I counted reluctantly, "FOO-AAA-UUR!"

Clutching my arms tightly across my chest, I winded myself.

"Drama queen!"

I was not acting, not now. I was a real drama queen. The play was just pretend.

As Lewis Carroll surfaced from down the aisle, passing fawning audience members on the way, the play began. The curtain dragged itself up and I walked into view.

"Look at the clock! Remember, Alice, eyes above the audience."

Drama for real. Legs shaking, dress encumbering every movement, I was greeted by a medley of well-rehearsed sighs. Tearing my eyes away from the floorboards, un-nailing them with my will, I raised them towards the clock. Disobeying me, my eyes focused themselves on a shiny bald patch, seated a few rows down from the refreshments stall. My own parents sat a few seats further forward. My sisters squirmed, bored and embarrassed, behind their programmes.

As a young child, Dad had warned me against being the centre of attention. In defiance, I had craved all the attention I could get. Drama queen. I had wanted to be looked at, to be listened to, to be heard, to be noticed. I wanted to be there in everyone's eyes, in everyone's ears, in everyone's faces. I wanted to scream at everyone who ignored me. I wanted, more than anything, to be the centre of attention. Now, my wish had come true. Dad would have said, "What you wish for and what you get are often very different things."

I was in the spotlight. I was Alice. My name was in the title: *Alice in Wonderland*. Today, I just wanted Wonderland with no Alice.

Woodenly, I seated myself on the grassy cardboard bank. Sitting poised, I mimed reading a book. *The Saint Annual* I had wished to convey in Shaun's interest had gone missing. Instead, I held a coverless spy story, hardbacked by plain red cardboard.

Unsure of note and pitch, I raised my voice to let it carry across the headtops. Sighing, I launched into the weary ballad of the title song: "Alice in Wonderland. How do you get to Wonderland? Over the sea or underland… Or just behind a tree? Where can it be?"

My "be" hit a peak, then dropped painfully into the pages of the spy book.

Applause dropped like dough.

Cheers rang out as the White Rabbit made his appearance. Running, this time with the vigour of an athlete, down the aisle through the seated shadows, he flung his oversized watch from side to side, face remaining deadpan throughout.

"I'm late! I'm late! For a very important date!"

"Curiouser and curiouser!" I exclaimed.

Alice struck me as being merely a vacuous observer of the Wonderland around her. She was merely the Victoria sponge beneath the eccentric, fascinating icing of strange characters that made up Wonderland.

Chasing the White Rabbit into the woods, I fell, twirling down into the warren. As Damon swirled the lighting effects, I spun my arms around like Wonder Woman. Leaping into a crumpled heap, I felt the set reveal itself behind me. Hand-painted to every small detail, the artistry of many was blurred, to the audience, by distance.

"Cats and rabbits," I sang, "would reside in fancy little houses. Dressed in shoes and hats and fancy trousers. In a world of my own."

Roisin cringed as I patted her rabbit ears.

"There'd be bluebirds. Lots of nice and friendly how-de-do birds… In a world of my own." A world of my own.

Oliver was in a world of his own. Smiling silently, skipping cat-suited to the piano, he was captivated by the music of the overhead lights. As each crimson star, each blue diamond, each silvery-green ray darted across his face, he swam in its colour.

Scenes flew past with the speed of the Rabbit's stopwatch, each act receiving greater applause. Washed away in a flood of Alice tears, I approached the scene of the Mock Turtle. *The Swimming Song* began.

Younger children entered the scene, linked securely between the collective hands of their captors. Gareth was absent. The little seahorse lost his costume as it was trampled beneath the feet of the dancers.

James shone as the Cheshire Cat, even if his nerves did allow him to twiddle. The Caterpillar, played by Barry, a staff member from the primary-age unit, received a number of fans from the audience.

Seating myself at the Mad Hatter's table, I encountered a raving Neil Proshka, face split horizontally by a manic grin. As he urged me over towards the gigantic teapot, he asked genially: "Would you like some tea?"

Drinking heartily from an empty plastic cup, I noticed the lack of a Dormouse within the structure. Elena was obviously unwilling to perform.

"No room! No room!" urged Sebastian as the March Hare, shouting his lines through constant prompting.

"Really?"

"Really O'Riley!" added the Hatter, improvising his own wit into the script. His fingers flickered into a twiddle.

"Twinkle, twinkle, little bat," sang Elena, making a late appearance, "How I won-der what yourat. Upabovetheskysohigh... Like a tear-tray inthesky."

Applause. Her parents in the audience added to the dour Christmas spirit in Elena's world. Soon, they would be leaving without her.

As Shaun and myself were arrested by a pack of human playing cards, we enjoyed a short conversation beneath the music.

"I found out what that record was on the radio the other day."

"Another obscure sixties band?"

"No. Seventies band. Gallagher and Lyle."

"Gallavant and Kylie?"

"Gallagher and Lyle. Gallavant and Kylie. Tate and Lyle sugar. It was called a *syrupy ballad* by the DJ. Imagine that! A ballad made of syrup. Each note must be dipped in syrup to give it added sickliness and sweetener, like saccharine, the stuff staff put in their tea."

Before I could mime putting my fingers down my throat, I remembered where I was. The conversation stopped abruptly.

"Gallagher and Lyle…"

"Off with her head!"

"OFF WITH HER HEAD!"

Confronted by the jury, I had no defence before the narrowed eyes of Calista. Dressed in her party dress, she looked strangely out of place for a juror.

"OFF WITH HER HEAD!"

"OFF WITH HER HEAD!"

My head never came off. Instead, I was whisked back to my grassy bank with a spin of the lights. Assembled, the cast sang *Winter Wonderland*.

"In the meadow we can build a snowman," sang Shaun, Neil, Simon and I, "And we can pretend he's Uncle Derek."

Nobody heard.

"Fairy 'cross the Mersey."

Uncle Derek merely tapped his tambourine with good cheer.

Stars of the show, we left the stage. My mother, giving me a hug, congratulated me on my performance, despite my bungle where I caught my foot in the curtain. My father nodded his head in approval. My sisters slunk out of sight, bewildered by the menagerie of Wonderlanders. Reaching for a cigarette, Mum savoured a glass of wine. Surveying the programme, Dad praised the skills of the White Rabbit. Nobody mentioned *The Swimming Song*.

Climbing into the car, I looked forward to Christmas with Lucy. I had bought her a large stocking filled with treats. A foxy-faced Golden Retriever, she had been the friend I had missed the most during my stay at Easton House.

Last Christmas, muddy and rain-soaked, she had spent the night at the bottom of my duvet, pleasantly crushing my legs against the winter chill. After leaving a new set of Crayola crayons on the carpet, I had woken up to find that they had vanished. Instead, they filled the stomach of my closest companion, making her quite ill. Normally when she was hungry, I would walk with her to the local shop where we would split a large bar of Dairy Milk between ourselves. She would plead for the sweet chocolate with her huge, brown eyes.

Waving to Shaun, I was stopped at the window by an unfamiliar member of staff: "I never knew you were a resident at Easton House. You verbalised those lines so well!"

Driving home, Wonderland disappeared behind me.

– TWELVE –

I WAS INVISIBLE.

Lost inside a hard, wooden shell, I pushed my knees towards my chest, quietly breathing, holding back the slightest cough or sigh that might betray me. Shifting sideways on the seat of my trousers, I felt the floor creak beneath my weight. Peering through the thin line of white light, I saw only the tiny view of wall and carpet in front of my eyes. Sucking small gasps of air into my lungs, I waited.

Sweating, I tried not to let the heat bother me, but heat seemed to radiate from my every pore. Breath moist and clammy, I could feel my hands grow slippery as I touched my face. Ears alert, eyes constantly drawn to the unmoving flash between the doors, I crouched beneath the clothes above my head.

As a coat slipped over my face, a tremor ran through my chest. Fumbling away from it, I was caught in the arms of a woollen cardigan. As my feet hit a pair of unlaced shoes, a deep rumbling groan came from inside the hollow. It was only the wood rubbing against the soles of my feet. Leaning back into the wall, I was forced to pull myself forwards.

A voice rang out from far away. The sound of frustration was carried in its shrill, untidy note. The pounding of feet and the shuffling of clothes passed by down the corridor. Shouts fell down the staircase, answered only by suspicions and mistakes. Relief, short lived, would soon flee also.

Earlier in the day I had refused to eat an apple. After coming back from the town centre in a hand-lock, due to purposefully straying from the group, I had added to my disobedience by muttering the name of a bovine mammal beneath my breath as my captor held me. Sybil, on hearing the obscenity, had forbidden me my Saturday chocolate biscuit, normally following the group picnic lunch. The picnic, however, had taken place within the dining room. I had been given mine last in the hope that I would repent whilst eating it. As I sat, pushed away from the table, with my miserable cheese sandwich instead of my usual tuna one, I was becoming a subject for discussion.

"Silly gurl! Silly gurl!" mocked Jonathan, prompted by Steff.

"Very, VERY silly girl!" added Sybil, biting into my intended tuna sandwich.

"Calista's not a silly girl!" shone Calista with a golden smile.

As her face beamed with sanctimonious one-upmanship, I had risen from my seat, hand curled in a fist. She pushed me further each time she gleamed at me from her chair.

"Bitch!" I spat.

"Move further away, then apologise!"

My chair was yanked back another metre.

As I fell from the speeding plastic, I fell on my knees to the floor, as if in submission. Caught in this pitiful pose, I rose to my feet. Why should I submit? I had already lost all there was I could have gained. Why submit just to make them happy? There would be no apologies and no remorse. Anger crushed repentance. I would be a bad loser. Any apology I could give would be false, and through gritted teeth. I wanted *them* to see how it felt to be the loser.

I would humiliate them, and at all costs.

As the apple, hard-skinned and bruised, had been placed on my plate I had moulded my face into a look of indifference before placing it, gently, back into the fruit bowl.

To eat it would be submission. I would baffle them first, then frustrate them. There would be no *sorry*. *Sorry* was merely a word to suggest that they had won. To say *sorry* would not be with honesty, but artificiality. Forced and unnatural, it was a word to brand the loser into subservience. It was nothing I would say. Whenever I had heard the word spoken inside Easton House, it was always added, mechanically, to the

end of a forced, meaningless sentence. The speaker rarely even understood why they were saying it.

Sorry was a lie.

The apple was placed, by the hand of Sybil, back onto my plate.
Once again I returned it to the fruit bowl.

"Eat it and apologise!"

I remained silent. The apple returned home.

"Eat it and apologise!"

This time the apple remained untouched.

"Now," said Sybil harshly, "I think it's time you said you were
sorry!"

Sorry. She had spoken the dreaded word. I was not sorry. If anyone
should be sorry, it was her. She had given me a burn on my wrist from
the hand-lock, she had humiliated me at the table and deprived me of
my privileges.

Pushing the apple away from me as though it were poison, I left it
uneaten.

"You're not going upstairs until you have finished your lunch! And
that means *eating* your apple!"

"It's not *my* apple," I retorted. "It doesn't belong to me."

"It does now!" snapped Sybil, losing her patience. "Eat it!"

"If it's *my* apple, then I can give it to *you*," I said, as if talking to a
child.

"No! It's YOURS!"

"If it belongs to me, then I can do what I want with it."

Already her cheeks were burning red, her small double chin quivering slightly with each argument. I was winning.

Turning to Steff, she spat the words: "Cheeky little bitch!"

Sybil was now down to my level. We were even. A glimmer of satisfaction spread through me as I felt the elation. Unfortunately it lasted a
mere few seconds as the subject of the apple was redressed.

Thumping the fruit down on my plate, adding more bruises to its
battered body, she locked my gaze with her eyes. Cold grey beneath
sticky, blue-tinged lashes, they resembled two lead bullets in mascara.

"You keep my apple!" I said with a flourish, watching her gold St Christopher rattle against my breath.

As she reached out to grab my red-ringed wrist, I tore my arm firmly from her grasp. Through blinkered vision, all I saw was the doorway and defiance. Leaping over the chair that stood in my way, I made my exit, followed closely by Sybil and Steff.

I was small, they were tall. I was flabby in places, but they were far flabbier. In truth, I could easily outrun them.

Pacing up the stairs, legs melting with each step, I swiftly turned a corner into my own bedroom. Surely they would find me there. However, I could hide within the room: a hiding place within a hiding place. I was hiding in such an obvious location that they would either find me straight away or ignore such a blatant, almost imbecilic scheme, expecting me to be more clever. Thus, I chose the wardrobe.

Through the narrow crack of illumination, I could see the shiny paper face of John Taylor. He was looking out for me, like a guardian angel. I knew I was protected: safe.

Closing my eyes, I imagined his presence beside me. The two of us would be together as fugitives, like Bonnie and Clyde.

The moment seemed to last for ever. On my watch it was half an hour.

Suddenly the door slammed open, crashing into the wall with fury. Behind it stood Sybil, ablaze. Seeing nothing in the room, she slammed back down the corridor.

Apples clouded my vision.

Safe, for that moment, I knew she would return. Once she discovered me, which would happen sooner or later, I would be put in the quiet room. If Sybil found me she would be the winner. I would be in the quiet room until I apologised.

She had now been searching long enough. Already she must be feeling humiliated. For her lack of guile, I hoped she looked all the more brainless to those who were free.

As she made another return to the room, I saw her moving towards the wardrobe. To defeat her, instead of surrendering on my discovery, I would reveal myself and mock her. I may be condemned to the quiet room for longer, but behind the door of solitary confinement, which was inevitable either way, I would be having the last laugh.

As she edged closer towards the wardrobe, I chose to move. Flinging open the door, I emerged from my concealment letting out a cry. Infuriated at my game, she seized me by the shoulders, pulling my arms behind my back into a hold. Struggling, I broke free, sliding under her wrists. Running from her towards the door, I was tripped as she grabbed me around the waist. For once, no time could be spared for play-acting. Instead of falling into my predictable faint, swoon or catatonic state, I merely writhed with all my strength. Unable to break her lock, I lifted my feet from the ground. Now she held my full body weight. Her hold loosened as I dropped to the floor. Scrambling away, I was pushed to the carpet with a blow from her elbow. No pretend bruises developed on my skin. The urge to run took me over.

Crawling on my knees stunned, I was in forced submission. This I detested, but I was unable to raise myself to my feet. Sybil was both larger and stronger than me. She could easily win on brute force.

"Cheeky bitch!"

"Get your hands off me, you fat cow!" I screamed with anger, dragging myself across the hurting floor.

"Quiet room!"

On impulse, I tripped her with my foot.

"Duvet!"

Panic overtook me as she dragged me down the stairs. Clinging on, like a drowning monkey, to the rail, my fingers reddened then whitened before being prised away. Static, I refused to move. Sybil used her knee to dislodge me from my space. Falling, my arms and legs left the carpet. Panic had replaced logic.

Crashing onto the landing, I felt the burns on my elbows and the pain in my back. Alerting Sybil to my injuries, she took them to be false. Enraged, she gave a signal to the waiting Steff.

I was duveted.

Half an hour later, still seething, I was unravelled towards the quiet room. As the door slammed shut, I tore at the woodwork with my fingernails, hoping to unnerve the two women waiting outside.

"Every swear word adds five minutes to your time!" warned Sybil, allowing Steff a coffee break.

Easton House contained two quiet rooms. One lay downstairs in wait behind Stacey's classroom. This quiet room had no lock and was boarded from behind by a large wooden supply cupboard. This cupboard had proved itself easy to move, making escape a simple operation. Simon, once contained for stealing pens and back-chatting to staff, had used this to his advantage. After moving himself to the corridor behind, he had escaped through the open front door, running joyfully down the street. Later he had been given a sheet of lines to do.

Upstairs lay a different sort of quiet room. This one had a lock. Each of its four walls was free of moveable furniture. The window was protected by a lattice of steel mesh.

Sometimes the quiet rooms were referred to as *time out rooms*. This phrase evoked images of people relaxing, reading newspapers and watching television. That was a deception.

"Fucking sadist!" I howled, kicking at the mesh. "You're fat, you're a bitch, and I don't think anyone here really likes you! I don't! None of my mates like you! Some of the other staff are fucking scared of you! *They* don't like you! They're just scared of you! You're a fat bitch!"

"Twenty minutes added for each of those!" she snapped before returning my string of insults: "If you'd *like* to know, I DO have friends. More than you'll ever have! *I* don't need to be watched all the time in a place like this! I have a husband, *and* a social life! Anyway, it's not fat. It's a baby!"

Taking a gulp of stale air, I debated whether to believe her. She was fat, but didn't look pregnant.

"You're in a fine position to talk," she continued. "YOU might think I'm fat and a bitch, but I've *never* been called ugly. Jessica! Can you hear me?" She paused before launching her next attack: "I've never been crap at sport. I was always picked first for the netball team. *I made an effort!* So, at school, I was definitely not *fat*. And my husband thinks I'm beautiful.

"I've never been dumpy or had a big nose like yours, or a big chin like yours, or an ugly little face like yours! You'll *never* have what I've got!"

The words came like those of a curse. Damning, they cut me worse than the carpet burns. I sank to the floor, sobbing. Tears replaced swear words.

Instead of wanting to destroy Sybil, I wanted to destroy myself. Tearing a nail scraping it down the door, I gave up. I had lost.

"Born to lose," I sobbed.

"No, you're not getting pity!" said Sybil. "You're the last person to deserve pity."

"I don't want pity. I want to get out."

"*I want* never gets!"

"Let me out! Let me out! LET ME OUT!"

"It doesn't seem very quiet in that quiet room," mused Steff, from outside, returning from her break.

A short, hushed discussion soon followed.

"If you can be quiet for ten minutes," offered Steff, "you can be out of the quiet room."

Trying to oblige, I stared, without remorse, at the wall. Neil, a regular visitor to the quiet room, had left his mark above the panelling. In his angular scrawl, he had written the legend: "BILL, BILL, FAT, FAT BILL. TO BILL COLLINS, AS IN PHIL COLLINS. BILL COLLINS FROM DUMBFORD IS BILL TUMFORD. BILL BUMFORD! A-HA! TO FAT BILL COLLINS OF DUMBFORD, FAT BUMFORD, TUMFORD TUMFORD!"

The word association continued in microscopic form. Surely he had already been caught for such poetic vandalism. I could almost hear the twiddling of his hands as he held the pen.

Bill Collins, nicknamed *Luke Fagsmoker*, due to his chronic nicotine addiction, was indeed portly, and the butt of many of Neil's jokes. Bill was notorious for singling out individuals, promoting some, such as Jonathan, to high positions like chief car-washer, whilst demoting others, like Neil, to being personal punchbags for his more stressful moments. In choosing Neil, he could only hope to add to his stress.

"Apologise and you can come out."

My lips refused to utter an apology.

"I want to hear an apology!" ordered Sybil.

I want never gets, I thought.

"I'd apologise now," advised Steff. "You don't want to be in there all night now, do you?"

"Sorry!" I spat, detesting the word as it sullied my tongue.

Sybil had won again.

As I surrendered, the door was opened. Stumbling outside in a red-eyed haze, I felt my legs tremble beneath me. I was handed a sheet of paper and a pen.

"I think you should write an apology to Sybil," Steff whispered loudly.

"I'll do it in my room," I lied.

"It would be better if you did it downstairs, whilst the others are enjoying the film."

Reluctantly, I headed towards the empty room downstairs. Saturdays were supposed to be fun days.

Turning on the light, I wasted time flicking through a few books. Shaun's "Bible" lay tucked in its usual place, scriptures of plane crashes and assassinations yellowed through exposure.

Upon the wall hung the same, familiar pictures. A few new ones had been added lately. Sebastian had produced several postmen and one fireman. Richie had contributed a dot-to-dot racing car, Sally a family-based piece entitled *The Outing*, Shaun a portrayal of Prague.

Prague was Shaun's favourite artistic destination. He only ever varied his talent over two subjects: Prague and President Kennedy's assassination, the latter a topic from which he was discouraged. However, when observing Shaun's masterpiece, in the corner a presidential assassin could clearly be seen.

"The Holy Bible!" I held it in my hands.

A Kennedy brother nearly drowned beneath my fingers. Shaun had acted out the scene once in the swimming baths. Shaun had left a crease in the corner. It was *his* book, which he shared, graciously, with Simon and me.

Footsteps sounded along the corridor, treading softly upon the carpet. They did not belong to either of the Amazon Twins.

Distinctly un-Amazonian, they belonged to Rosa Wittington. Behind her glasses, Rosa surveyed the empty sheet of paper. She was smaller than the dreaded Twins, middle-aged and slightly sad-featured. She was warm and sat down beside me at the desk.

"I think you'd better write something," she suggested. "Miriam's not well happy."

Sighing in her broad Geordie accent, she doubted the methods of her compatriots: "Once you've got this over with, there *might* be some supper left for you."

"I might not have any. I'm already fat: a size twelve."

Hungry from my earlier escapade, I fought off my cravings.

"Oh, I wouldn't worry about it at your age," she smiled with a nod. "I've been on a constant diet for over fifteen years."

Now in her late thirties, her weight had swung, between the years, from twenty stone to eight stone ten. She was no stranger to the torments of food.

"Do you think I'm fat?" I asked, revealing a swollen teenage belly.

"Ah, that'll go away with a little exercise," she suggested. "If you want, I'll ask Derek if tomorrow night you, me and a few others can do the exercise video."

Derek's wife had kindly donated *Jane Fonda's Workout* to Easton House.

"I wish I was as thin as Kylie," I sighed, reluctantly starting the first line of my apology letter.

– THIRTEEN –

MARVIN'S TREE STOOD majestically atop its mud-strewn bank as a monument to every barbecue, sports event and alfresco meal that occurred in the garden. With its tall, branchless back pressed firmly against the wall, it spread out its narrow branches to the neighbours. Singular scraps of torn paper adorned its lanky figure, hanging from each scrawny twig like colourless bunting. Stones gazed up from its feet in awe.

Marvin's Tree had been, unofficially, christened by Simon after he had seen a departed staff member once try to climb it. Needless to say, he had failed in his attempt. However, the name held a certain sentiment in the hearts of Easton House and, thus, it had stuck.

Today, the entirety of the staff and young people had assembled in the garden for evening break. A few stayed indoors, such as Elena, who was on a new programme, and Sybil who was assisting her.

Shaun had brought his guitar outside, reluctantly leading the sing-song. In between each number, he would revert to his old favourite: *Needles and Pins* by The Searchers. Sometimes he would play a clever, neat little intro, before chopping and changing into segments of various other songs. This irritated Eva greatly.

Shaun, normally late downstairs for breakfast, had gone missing that morning. Both the bathroom and the corridor had been searched. Half an hour had passed. He was eventually discovered in, of all places, his own bedroom! Seated, cross-legged and naked on the bed, he had caused Uncle Derek a severe trauma to his modest mind. In his hands, he had been holding his guitar, gently strumming the melody of *Needles and Pins*.

"I saw her today. I saw her face," he sang in his monotone voice. "It was the face I loved…"

Merrily, Simon added to the chorus and Peter Samson provided a buzzing bassline through his coat-toggles.

Earlier, I had read the rota, being now privileged to do so. Predicting the outdoor sing-song (it normally happened when Uncle Derek supervised the breaks), I had prepared a small vocal group in the female bathroom. Whilst Sally, Dale and myself had been washing our hands, I had taken advantage of their echolalia, prompting them with the lyrics to Duran Duran's *Rio*. Sabrina already knew them – after all, I had inflicted my music on her at break too often.

"Shaun! *Rio!*"

Quickly, I assembled the singers.

"A-one-two-three-FOUR!"

Discordantly, we began: "Her name is Rio and she dances on the sand…"

Impressed, Eva began to clap. Aside from her support, there was little to be won. As the vocalists forgot the melody, I found myself singing alone. Hanging like a thin thread of brown cotton, my voice trailed away into the tangled knot of the chorus.

"Not much sand around here to dance in!" added Wayne. "It's all full of petrol."

"Do *your* song!" requested Eva to Shaun, Simon, myself and the, now silent, figure of Peter. "The *Biblical* song."

"About the Big Book," whispered Shaun.

"A-one-two-three-FOUR!" we counted as Simon and I picked up tennis rackets.

"Cyril Smith, every inch a liberal…" quoted Shaun from the Big Book. "Streaker at the pitch at Twickenham!"

Each headline came flooding through our vocal chords.

"John Derry, about to set a record…" my voice fell uncomfortably low. "But unfortunately his plane ploughed into the crowd."

"Dum! Dum!" added Peter on vocal percussion.

"Loads o' smooooke!" echoed Simon, jauntily swinging his long legs over the bench. "From jets hijacked in Jordan…"

Shaun and I, the lyricists, had argued over the inclusion of that line. Personally, I had wanted to substitute something about the Queen. Much of the second verse was voiced solely by Shaun and Simon.

"Don Campbell, his boat did flip."

Don Campbell, the record-breaking speedboat racer, had been thrown mid-air from his vessel, Bluebird, in 1967. According to the Book, his body was never discovered.

"Der-der-der with a little bin liner, looking a right proper drip."

Der-der-der was my substitute for the name *John Taylor*. A thieving groundsman caught smuggling stolen goods, he could never be mistaken for my synonymous idol.

As the song ended, chuckles were outnumbered by blank faces. Uncle Derek gave a nod of disapproval. Eventually, he requested the more appropriate *Sing a Rainbow*, official anthem of Easton House. Led by the charms of Sally, the singing group grew louder.

The sing-song gradually drew to a close and, to everybody's joy, the bikes were wheeled from the shed. Amongst them was a BMX, which Shaun took for his own. Whilst choosing for myself a flat-tyred racer, I found myself contemplating the fate of Don Campbell.

A figure appeared at the window. Inside the building, Elena would be busy earning her next food-task.

Instead of meals, Elena was given several food-tasks per day. For her, it was a task, not only to dress and wash herself appropriately, but to eat appropriately, if at all. Usually, these small meals consisted of a sandwich and a glass of Complan. This "pink milk" was her favourite beverage.

"Pink milk!" she called, poking her head through the doorway. "Pink milk! Eat nana drink pink milk!"

Hysterically, she began to laugh, her entire body shaking with each giggle.

Inside the domestic science room, she would be mixing the Ribena and cordial whilst Miriam cut the fruit.

Fifteen minutes later, Miriam brought out two large jugs on a tray. Behind her, Elena carried the plastic cups.

"Sorry about the fruit salad," apologised Miriam to Uncle Derek, "but Elena ended up adding a little too much Ribena. I decided we'd have fruit punch instead."

Accepting her pink milk, Elena noticed that the glass was half empty.

"Big pink milk!" she requested.

"You would've got a full glass," scolded Miriam, "if only you'd been more careful with the Ribena!" Mercifully, she added: "If you sit quietly and be good, you'll get the other half at supper."

"Be good?"

"That's right. *Then* you'll get your pink milk."

Sipping the first glass of fruit punch, Neil winced. Simon, served second, spat his out onto the grass.

Swiftly, Eva confiscated his glass.

"Who took a sickly drink off Peter?" asked Shaun, mocking his deputy.

"Bet it was you!" called Simon.

"Bet it was you!" called Shaun.

"Bet it was you!"

"Bet it was you!"

"BET IT WAS YOU-HOO!" chorused the duo in harmony.

"Peter Samson took his own drink off 'imself!" added Simon, giving the final verdict.

"What does a sickly drink taste of?" prompted Shaun, trying the wit of Simon on for size.

"Sick," replied Simon. "Oh, sick, but with bits of fruit in it."

"Why don't you two just shut up?" called Eva, tiring of their conversation.

"Shut up..." mused Neil, joining the discussion. "Shut up, sit up...syrup, syrup. SYRUP!"

"Syrup!" cried Simon. "That Peter Samson 'ad better syrup or 'e'll be getting into trouble! Trouble from me an' Uncle Derek!"

"Syrup," pondered Shaun. "The same syrup used by Gallagher and Lyle in their syrupy ballad?"

"Shaun! Simon!" warned Uncle Derek. "Are you two being obsessional with your chatter? If you are, I shall have to split you up. One of you can sit with Eva."

A few lines of dialogue later, Eva came to sit between them.

"Now, Shaun," she scolded, "if I hear anything about music, or if I hear the words *James* and *Bond* mentioned together, I'll have to keep you and Simon separated."

Glumly, Shaun cast his eyes to the ground. Ian Fleming's greatest creation had not been mentioned since teatime, which had been two hours ago.

Simon, meanwhile, had lambasted Peter Samson with various accusations throughout the evening.

"And, Simon," she warned, "you and Peter sleep in separate bedrooms now, so I suggest you stop mentioning him."

"Sorry," muttered Simon, before breaking into a grin.

– FOURTEEN –

DEACON HAZELDENE LOVED peanut butter. A connoisseur of the deliciously ground paste of many fortunate nuts, he chose the crunchy variety above the smooth. Spreading a thick, golden layer onto a substantial wedge of toast, he sighed a huge, passionate "Mmmmm!" before taking a well-earned mouthful. Licking the sticky, golden tar from his teeth, his tongue savoured this delicacy, the sacrifice of each individual peanut being heavily appreciated. Folding the malted mattress of kibbled toast into a taco, he licked away all escapees from his chin.

Clapping his hands on finishing the delights, he applauded himself over his accomplishment.

Athletically trained, broad-shouldered and handsome, Deacon had spent less than a week at Easton House. Already, he was making a name for himself. Running in large, circular orbits around the garden sundial, he would convey his physical prowess with great pride. Fifteen years old, hazel-eyed and tall, he would receive admiring glances from females in the supermarket. Often, gazing over their shopping baskets in awe, they would then stand, mystified, as he licked the floor.

Deacon, for reasons known only to himself, liked to lick. Be it kitchen floors, turf lawns, concrete paving stones, or even the carpet of his own bedroom, he would somehow find himself unable to fight this urge. Causing great puzzlement to those who encountered him, this habit was both bizarre and satisfying.

Nobody, not even Deacon, knew how this habit had been formed, or even the exact purpose of it. Often rising from his chosen surface

with a large grin of fulfilment, this licking seemed strangely reward-
ing. As those around him merely stood baffled, Deacon would express,
in his face, a sense of knowing.

Did he know why he licked? Maybe only a part of him did.
Perhaps his licking ruled over him, without him even realising it.
Maybe it was his habit, not himself, that did the licking.

Aside from licking, Deacon liked to jump. Becoming excited, he
would leap uncontrollably into the air, pogo-ing without refrain. This
had earned him the nickname *Zebedee*.

Like licking, jumping was a great source of satisfaction in Deacon's
life. Both, however, seemed compulsory. Both were spontaneous and
could happen at inopportune moments in a number of different places.
Often, a single lick or jump could raise great concern within the staff.
Sometimes he would smile whilst in action. Often, he was labelled a
wind-up merchant due to these outbursts. Often, peanut butter could
curb these urges.

Keen on motorcycles, although never having rode one himself,
Deacon would imitate the burr of a buzzing engine. Whilst running
circuits, his motor would rev and hum as he picked up speed. Sometimes, in the swimming baths, he would become a speedboat, trailing
the spray of white water behind him as he spun his propellers.

Standing almost six feet tall, he looked all the larger for his build.
Often, as a friendly gesture, he would tap smaller, usually female, staff
members on the crown. When anxiety ruled, the knocks became
harder. On some occasions, he had come close to stunning his victims.

At weekends, a small group would assemble before lunch to watch
the Grand Prix. Deacon, buzzing like the tyres of the combined
Formula One racers, would be accompanied by Simon's rousing commentary. Peter, meanwhile, would announce the start, the finish, the
winner and the losers. Waving his hand in the motion of a flag, Peter
would then encourage Deacon to "drive".

The Scalextric provided a great source of Saturday entertainment.
Simon, perpetually the red car, red being his favourite colour, would
race with determination against Deacon. His opponent would take the
yellow car. If a car flew from the tracks, each racer would be sure to

place it back carefully, Simon occasionally moving his slightly ahead of Deacon's.

Roisin had taken a shine to Deacon. Usually, he would sit in her classroom flicking through each book on transport, pointing out to her each Harley Davidson or Honda. Together, they had decided, they would each buy a motorbike: complete with chrome hubcaps and side-car. They would tinker around with each bike before finally hitting the open road. Unfortunately, neither had the money. However, Roisin's old car was often admired by her eager companion. Standing beside the Austin Metro, Deacon would point out each small detail in the exhaust pipe or gear-stick, before bending over to look underneath.

Eunice, normally tired and jaded from driving the bus or preparing the picnic, would be assured of a hug for her efforts. As he embraced her, Deacon would let out a soft, sustained "Aaaaaaah!".

A great purveyor of peanut butter in all its forms, crunchy, smooth, sweetened or unsweetened, Eunice formed a strong bond with her worthwhile comforter.

Inside the large bedroom that housed the collective of Deacon, Simon, Peter, Sebastian and Richie, the walls were adorned with posters. Most of these belonged to Deacon. In between the dot-to-dot animals of Richie and the uniformed characters of Sebastian sat a large, glossy motorbike. Beneath it were various wrestlers, Arnold Schwarzenegger and Guns N' Roses. Simon had placed some of the wrestlers next to his bed. An Airfix model car often changed sides during the night.

Sometimes, when excited, Deacon would come running down the corridor, ignoring the warnings of Uncle Derek over the dangers of speed, hurling himself through the double doors before shouting: "Deacon rides a motorbike! Yeah!"

Most of Deacon's sentences began with his Christian name before ending in a loud "Yeah!".

"Deacon go splash-paddle-motor-boat on the seaside yeah!"

He would often repeat his favourite: "Deacon eat peanut butter yeah! Deacon eat belly get bigger-bigger-bigger-bigger-bigger-

BIGGER...BANG! YEAH! Deacon been licking, peanut butter sandwich gets smaller-smaller-smaller..." Here, his voice grew tiny: "...smaller-smaller...GONE! Yeah!"

Not only was Deacon a star motor-mimic, athletic pogo-ist and loyal devotee of peanut butter, but he was also a superhero: a superhero by the name of *Duvetman*.

This title had been awarded as I had watched him lumber, slowly, across the landing before lolling about on a retired duvet. Comfortably, he had wrapped himself up in its, usually ominous, form, before rolling and humming across the carpet. Eventually growing tired of this motion, he had unravelled himself before placing the duvet nobly across his shoulders like a cloak. Spreading his arms wide and aloft, he took flight down the corridor, billowing white cape streaming out grandly behind him.

Together, Shaun and I had written him a theme tune. To the familiar melody of the *Spiderman* theme, we sang: "Duvetman, Duvetman! Does whatever a duvet can! Wrap him up! Let him out! Let's hear everybody shout...DUVETMAN!"

Soon, to all the young people, the duvet became a strangely less threatening concept.

— FIFTEEN —

STERNOAKE HALL LOOMED ahead, towering like some square-cut, brick-walled modern citadel over the streets of the city. Half secluded by barbarous trees, its army of shrubs seemed liable to betray its tall, grey supremacy with their unruly branches. As Eva left the bus to prise open the iron gates, rotting beneath a thick layer of peeling blue paint, some of this man-made lichen rubbed off onto her fingers. Wiping her hand on the leg of her jeans, she cast her eyes over what was to be our new home. I knew. To the others, save for Shaun and Simon, today was just another day-trip, albeit a rather gloomy one.

It used to be a hospital, she informed me. Since its closure it had been waiting for its renewal, to be re-inhabited after years, how many is unknown, of standing derelict. Behind the overgrown foliage, its glass-eyed rooms seemed to watch us, blindly, cobwebs forming cataracts. Standing in the still air beneath the doorway, the breeze seemed comatose. I could feel it breathe a tired welcome through the decayed wooden skin of the door.

Pouring out from the stationary vehicle, the eager visitors took it upon themselves to explore. Today was an adventure: a *real* adventure.

"Don't get lost…"

Heading towards the forest, selecting fallen leaves at random from the undergrowth, Richie put half in his mouth and half in his pockets for later. He savoured their earthy texture, chewing each crumbling flake until his lips were brown. Simon, snatching away the morsels, tapped a warning finger of authority.

"Leaves don't taste good! You should eat pizza instead!"

As Uncle Derek turned the key, Sternoake Hall was weakly resur-
rected. A clamour arose, following him inside.

Inside the shell, we felt the musty corridor breathing dust from its
tar-filled lungs. Supporting the darkness were missing floorboards and
rusty nails. Scratching my thumb on a homeless screw, I saw above my
head a plaque veiled in brown. A tribute to the founders. It remembered, vaguely, somebody who had lost whatever little fame they had
through opening the place. The walls, painted a colour now unidenti-
fiable, were decorated with various blossoms of cracked plaster. Like
liver spots on ageing skin, they sat like the mottled decay on deceased
elderly flesh.

Sombrely, I trod across a stray piece of wood, barely afloat in the
void. Beneath me lay a mass, not quite the dramatic black, more a dull
opaque grey, like a bottomless puddle. Dull, unseeing, it was merely a
space filled with brick and rubble. Small stones rolled beneath my
shoes, tipping themselves lethargically over the edge. A dead plant
rose, like a sickly phoenix, from the debris.

Skipping from a loose plank to a stable slab of concrete, I pushed
open a door. Palms black from its touch, my prints remained off-white
against soot-peppered grey. A huge plague of germs would soon be
eating away at my forearms.

Awakening the room inside, I noticed, flecked across the bare floor,
small blue bars, like hospital soap. Simon, following me inside, picked
one up.

"Eeeurgh!" he choked, manipulating the blue thing with his
fingers. "Feels like Silly Putty!"

Shaun, taking a bar for himself, examined the substance more
closely.

"Rodenticide," he muttered, a slight smile coming to his lips.

"Rat poison?"

Staring at the innocent-looking bars in the hands of Shaun and
Simon, I found myself wondering if the poison was still active. It had
come into contact with their skin. Perhaps it would penetrate the epi-
dermis to the arteries and veins beneath, engaging itself into the
nervous system before disabling it, eventually causing death. Shaun

and Simon might die, I feared. Hopefully, the poison would not be strong enough. They might stand a chance. Watching their hands and faces, I feared the worst, should either lick their fingers by mistake. Surely the toxins would work faster that way.

"I'd keep my hands in my pockets," I warned them.

If Shaun and Simon fell victim, our little gang, now named *The Deadly Quartet*, would be cut down to just Peter Samson and me, rendering us a mere desolate duo.

The Deadly Quartet always had a taste for danger and the taboo. This week, before our visit to Sternoake Hall, the four of us had been caught, fully aware, in the attic behind the bedroom closet: the closet only inches away from my infamous wardrobe. Concealed behind a panel was a large hole punched into the wall, leading to our subterfuge hideaway.

Inside the dark attic, amongst the soot and rubble, we would bring various chemicals from the downstairs classrooms. Sharing the loot of Magic Markers, Tipp-Ex thinner, glue, poster paint and the odd aerosol that tumbled from our pockets, we would indulge ourselves in these friendly toxins, releasing ourselves from the grind of the rota. AWOL from the communal routine, we would inhale various gases, painting our senses with white delights and sticky surprises. Shaun got his chance to "re-live the Sixties", although he had not been born until the early Seventies. The rest of us merely enjoyed the escape and anonymity.

Inside our sooty-bricked womb of secrets, we lived our own universe. Unafraid of the filthy surroundings due to the joyful release of Tipp-Ex thinner, I wondered what such delights smelt of. Squatted in the corner, sullying the seat of his jeans, Shaun would entertain us with yarns from the world of Bond. As he was older and experienced in the art of espionage, we elected him our president. As our benevolent leader, he would head our small, Bohemian revolution behind the hushed walls of our stronghold.

Several times we had gone missing. At the moment we arrived at Sternoake Hall, we knew it would be an ideal place for disappearing in.

"Lost in Spaaaaaaace!"

Once, Elena had been abducted in the arms of Shaun and spirited to our attic hideaway. Strangely, she had enjoyed her role as his hostage, constantly giggling as he gently tickled her shoulders.

On the rota, her name, along with mine, had been marked down for embroidery. All the girls were subjected to embroidery, although most seldom enjoyed it. Eventually, Shaun's tickling had grown into petting. Elena had followed him of her own free will. Embroidery could wait.

"It's the hard stuff!" remarked Shaun, sniffing the rodenticide in his hands.

Removing the blue bar from its white card shelter, he twisted it around his thumb. Skilfully rolling it into a pear-shape in his palm, he then placed it in his back pocket. As his face curled into an expression of deep satisfaction, his eyes showed greater motives than simple self-intoxication.

"Know what I'll do?" he whispered, knowing that no staff were present. "I'm gonna put this blue stuff in Norris's cooking...in the soup. Then all the staff can eat rat poison and we'll all be free! We can steal the bus, Simon can drive, and escape!

"The plan is this: me and Simon put this stuff in the pot in the kitchen, when Norris the Cook isn't looking, whilst Sammo goes off it, distracting the staff! Meanwhile, you can be lulling them into a false sense of security, just to get the attention away from the kitchen. Cover us and act as back-up if anything goes wrong. I dunno...lie for us. Say we're adding curry spices to the broth."

"But you don't want to kill *all* the staff, do you?" added my conscience.

"No. Save Damon and Vince."

"What about Marie? I mean, she's Damon's wife and our mate."

"Not mine," protested Shaun. "She made me and Simon stay indoors for flooding the bathroom."

"Can we not save her anyway? And Roisin. Roisin needs saving."

"No. They'll tell everyone about our plot if we spare them."

"Shaun. If we spare *anyone*, how are we gonna save them if the poison goes in the big pot? I mean, everyone has to eat the same stuff at dinner."

"We'll warn them. Discreetly."

"Oh?"

"If they tell, then things become complicated. You'll have to defend us with a few words here and there."

"Right. I'll vouch for you."

I ended the conversation, almost ruefully, with images of prisons and police cars thudding through my head.

Deep inside, I knew that Shaun's conspiracy was just another fantasy. He was a man of words, not a man of action.

Voices shuffled outside our poisonous chamber. Discreetly, I obliged to Shaun's instructions and gently placed the tempting bar of blue evil inside the back pocket of my jeans. Later, I reassured myself, I would remove it.

Lagging behind the expedition, we followed the others up the main stairway, onto the landing. Running my, already soiled, hand over the large, ornately crooked figurehead of the bannister, I felt the soft lump against my flesh. Shuddering, I could feel its venom seeping through the denim onto my skin. Three of us already were plague-carriers, myself included. Beneath the papery white skin of my wrist, I could see the branches of my veins and arteries: a thin blue tree carrying poisonous blood into my system. My pulse seemed to grow louder, the fevered blood desperate to reach my brain. My heart was probably already corroded.

Wandering from the trodden route, I opened a bottle-green doorway to reveal a new, smaller, steeper stairway, leading into darkness. Treading cautiously onto the first step, I began to climb. Suddenly, from behind, a large shadow became solid, knocking against my shoulder, almost felling me to the floor. Looking ahead, I saw Deacon overtaking me, disappearing into the void without fear. Running into invisibility, soon only his feet were visible.

As there grew less and less of Deacon to be seen, a large crowd of concern gathered at the doorway. Uncle Derek, preferring to remain as comforter, remained on the lower ground as Trevor elected himself hero of the hour.

Trevor, a tall, plump man, was a source of both dread and amusement. Relatively new to the numbers of staff, he was already among Uncle Derek's elite: a fully-fledged member of the Quality Street Gang. Opposed to the Deadly Quartet and all of its intentions, he played a comic villain in his role, savouring it to the extreme. In keeping, his very appearance was comical. His head, curiously shaped like a Packham's pear, rested neckless on his fleshy, rounded shoulders, upper lip adorned by a neatly trimmed black moustache. Sleek and oily, it sat like a sleeping pet rat, sullenly guarding the flawless white of his smile. Atop his nose perched a small pair of round glasses, through which he surveyed each individual is if through a magnifying-glass.

Normally when on duty, he would enter his shift in a cleanly washed, freshly starched and ironed, white shirt: courtesy of his lovely wife, Cheryl. One of his white shirts was patterned with thin, pink stripes: a reminder of his former job as a senior worker at McDonalds. Apparently, he had dressed as Ronald McDonald a few times for children's parties and been quite enthusiastic to do so.

Flailing in his heroism, he struggled down the stairs with Deacon at his wrist. Eventually, he emerged to a flutter of applause. Shaun, standing silent at the back, had already marked Trevor down as one of his first victims.

Coronation Street shone through the dust at our feet, stars long gone or departed greeting us with friendly smiles from the bar of The Rover's Return. The paper, dated 17th August 1970, was *The Sun*. Shaun, reaching down for his souvenir, was denied by the hand of Trevor. Gritting his teeth, he vowed to return for these relics. He would hide them alongside his sticky blue weapon.

"I've got freedom in my pocket," he whispered.

Wandering down the next corridor, alone from both the group and my beloved Quartet, I glanced through each open door. Rusty old nursing scales greeted me from behind faded white desks. This decayed office had once belonged to a nurse. Once, before the dust had spoiled its hygiene, it would have been a formidable white temple to health and safety. Reminders of 1970 ran past as patients were aided into beds and doctors wrote out reports. Everything was ominously shiny: polished, disinfected, chemically engulfed. Stethoscopes and thermometers hung in various nooks and crannies. Drips hung pumping out sustained life whilst trolleys of food and coffee wheeled across clean tiles on creaking wheels. Pensioners read periodicals whilst sipping from plastic cups.

Germs had won the war against chemicals.

Through the carefully boarded window, I could see strands of the city outside. Cars raced, fuming, around a paradise road-island. Trees were huddled in the centre, reaching towards the sky for release. Schoolchildren squabbled outside the ivory gates of the convent beneath the weary gaze of a disapproving Virgin. Droves of students trudged past in a uniform of misdemeanour, drunken from more than just the heat. An old green jalopy spewed a cloud into the faces of a young couple walking the pavement. The sun, choked by dust, fled behind the roof of Siamese twin bedsits.

Causing the concave floor to groan beneath my feet, I reached down, pulling a scrap of newspaper from under the protruding tongue of the carpet. Rooting down further, I found a caricature I had drawn earlier of Trevor on the bus, his Packham's chin quadruple the size of his diminished forehead. Beneath the gargantuan face, scrawled in tiny blue letters, was a yarn from Shaun. Rolling it up into a quill, I signed random initials into the dust: Z.V. 1969.

Erasing my artwork, I recoiled at my own mistake. If a certain Z.V. had been present at the windowsill in 1969, surely the initials would have been erased long ago by more falling dust. Instead, I scrawled a large, elaborate D.Q. 1991.

Lumbering into the room in sensible shoes came Sabrina. Standing on the nursing scales, she was aided by Eva.

"Eleven stone! This thing must be bust!"

Unable to resist flapping across the floorboards, Sabrina was warned of the danger before being led back outside to the group.

BANG! KER-POW!

A rusty steel pipe hit me between the eyes.

"Don't move! I got a gun to your face!"

Peter Samson held the tool firmly in his hands. Pulling his hood down over his face, he made a sinister figure.

"STOP! I gotta gun!"

Earlier this morning, he had been caught with Shaun and Simon flooding the bathroom. In self-defence, he had picked up an aerosol can, entertaining this stunt with the unimpressed Trevor.

Putting down the "gun", he picked up a large plank of wood, swinging it around like a battleaxe.

"Don't shoot! Don't shoot!" he ordered all present.

"BANG! BANG! BANG!" added Simon, his opponent, carrying a useless exhaust-pipe: probably from an ambulance.

A small fight broke out before both gunslingers were reprimanded by Uncle Derek.

Inside what remained of the bathroom was a huge, white bathtub. Only the cold tap worked, the only running water in the entirety of the building.

"Submarine?" suggested Peter. "Stingray! STINGRAAAY!"

"'Iding place, more like," said Simon with approval, climbing inside to conceal his lanky frame.

Meanwhile, Shaun searched the cupboard. Disappointed, he found nothing, save for another predictable bar of rodenticide.

"Never find us 'ere!" remarked Simon.

This place was soon to be our new home. Easton House had only just grown comfortable and now I, like the others, would be moving on to this larger building. Easton House looked like what it was: a house, despite the fact that it was actually a residential school. Sternoake Hall, however, looked like what it had once been: a hospital. Official and efficient beneath its layers of age, I could already picture the kitchen in stainless steel, the bathrooms newly fitted with Armitage Shanks, shimmering from daily disinfection.

There were no peculiar quirks to the place at all, save for the relics of newspaper and bars of rodenticide. Each room was a neatly uniformed rectangle: straight and unwarped. No unusual décor framed the architecture and no carved features stared from the doorway. Neat, economical.

Soon there would be desks in the classrooms, new windows installed with double-glazing, a panel cut out of the kitchen wall for a dinner-hatch, colourless carpets that would match the magnolia-white walls.

Outside, the forest hid the interesting things. Soon, even that would be pruned for a safer environment.

Emerging from the bushes, Simon appeared at the helm of a wheel-barrow. Having lain concealed in the undergrowth for so long, it seemed to throw off its rust at this new opportunity for attention. Laughing, Simon crashed it into a tree.

As the bus drove away, the wheelbarrow returned to its resting place and Sternoake Hall awaited our return.

− SIXTEEN −

SITTING IN THE kitchen watching a nameless film I had seen many times before, I yawned slowly as the adverts took control. Making myself a glass of cordial, I heard the phone ring. Dad answered it.

"Who was it, Dad?"

"You jammy devil!" he grinned back.

"What?"

"You jammy, jammy devil!"

Dumbstruck, I guessed I must have won some competition or other. Maybe I would be rich, or have my name in the papers! Perhaps I had been given a part in a film, or the chance to appear in a music video! Maybe I had won a modelling contract, despite being a little too short. Maybe my bad skin, weight gain and awful teeth had been overlooked.

"You jammy, jammy devil!"

"What?"

"You…" he pointed with aplomb, "you are going to the Lake District…camping!"

"Camping?"

"Camping!"

Never before had I been camping, and never before had I wished to. This phone call merely enhanced my desire *not* to go camping. Not ever. Picturing a cold, windy hillside filled with sheepish rows of battered tents, I shuddered at the thought of such a "holiday".

"Do I *have* to go camping?"

"Well, everybody else from Easton House is…"

"Do I *have* to?"

"If I had the chance, I'd give my eye-teeth to go!"

Had it been allowed, I would have sent Dad in my place.

"You're going to the Lakes," he said with an uncharacteristic flourish. "It'll be great! You know, it's a great place, the Lakes."

He then proceeded to describe the delights of pleasant, airy countryside and the historic monuments that populated the rustic scenery. No amount of ruins or daffodils could persuade me to sleep under a draughty canvas sky. All I could recall of the Lake District was that it rained a lot. Wordsworth must have been an incredible propaganda merchant, I thought, also remembering how much I disliked his poetry.

"If I were you…"

"If you were me…"

"I would go and see Ullswater. Beautiful place. I went camping there once, when I was still a student."

Pondering over to rest her head in my lap, Lucy sensed that something was wrong. She could read the anxiety in my face with her huge, seal-like eyes. Glancing up woefully, she knew the both of us would be missing each other for a long time. Two weeks would seem even longer in the Lake District.

Katherine, my middle-younger sister, was slightly envious. Leslie, the youngest, just sighed and wished me a good time, probably wanting a holiday herself. This would not be a holiday, I thought, it was a punishment, for spending too much time behind closed doors.

I enjoyed spending time behind closed doors. Uncle Derek, fond of leading his "Welly Walks" out through the Dales, would often pity the likes of Eva and me as lightweights for our dislike of the open air. Uncle Derek's walks were seen as a privilege to all young people and a benefit of being in the Quality Street Gang: the unforgettable opportunity to leave the clammy confines of the building and indulge in nature's bounteous delights across wild, rambling country terrain.

Single, or perhaps double, file, the hardy wanderers would trail across the mud-soaked footpath of the Dene, signposts hanging gloomily over what was now a long, winding river of trodden boot-marks. Uniformed in compulsory matching cagoules, feet encased in layers of sporting cotton, protected impeccably by sweaty wellington boots, moisture sliding from their impenetrable surface into the void between boot and leg, the walkers would rarely hasten to stop, such was their desire to conquer the hill already claimed by a middle-aged couple with their dog.

Instead of undertaking such a challenge, Eva and I had formed a bond over our love of bargain-hunting at the market. Shaun would often accompany our little group of lightweights, scouring the record stalls for everything from Telly Savalas 45s to David Soul 33⅓s. Calista, afraid of the wind that blew apart her curls, would bide her time in the adoring eyes of the make-up stall holder. Garnished with strings of plastic pearls and crowned with tortoiseshell slides, she would hurriedly search her purse for change. Meanwhile, the rain would whip down over the market, streaming over the canvas roofs of each temptation.

For two entire weeks the residents of Easton House would be homeless. The building had already been sold, during the summer holidays, and Sternoake had already been bought. However, the new place was still enduring repairs, the builders being particularly slow in their progress, and we were now condemned to a "camping holiday".

Packing my cases, I waited with reluctance. After two weeks, I would probably stink.

Slowly passed the journey through the hills. As the hills turned into mountains, looming over our tiny bus as if to crush it, my mind slowly came awake. Huge boulders, big enough to flatten a small family, lay stationary on the slopes, lunging as if to roll into the roadside. Dark clouds poured deep-grey curtains of rain across the distant sunny backdrop of the sky. My mother painted landscapes. I could see her holding the entire scene on a canvas, rather like God, adding licks of trees and rock-face with her brush.

Behind me, Shaun contemplated disaster. Was it possible the bus could collide with a landslide? Was it possible for the bus to drive over a crumbling bridge before tumbling into the river? Once washed downstream, would it sink, or float a while in the current? If hit by a rock, would it burst into flames?

This was not the Dene, or even the Dales. This was the Lake District. No land was flat. Instead, the slopes of the gargantuan peaks seemed to move with the eyes, such was their immensity. Almost painfully, the earth seemed to be pulled skywards by some sinister force, lumps and bumps rising and falling like tsunamis of tormented land-flesh.

As the road vanished beneath the wheels, I watched them paint thick, black tracks across the gravel. Soon they would be gone, washed away by falling rain.

Uncle Derek, regarding each signpost to save in his memory, planned a walk for every day. Marie, offering to help mount the tents, was already an expert in such activities. Shaun, finding any opportunity to do nothing but think his thoughts, would hold the pegs in his hand, occasionally placing one or two into the pockets of Simon.

Pooley Bridge trundled into sight. A large, green field stretched behind the fence. Most of the resident campers were packing away for fear of the encroaching cold. On the grassy roadside, two elderly hikers smiled away the miles.

Birds flew under the moving bus. Untarnished, they escaped through the gap.

Surprisingly quickly, the tents were erected. Barry, senior of the junior school unit, greeted us with wide arms.

"Which tent will the girls be sleeping in?" asked Eva.

"That big one there, across from the boys."

"And which tent am I in?" I asked, absent-mindedly losing the conversation.

"Ah!" grinned Barry, patting me uncomfortably atop the head. "Ah! You'll be sleeping in that blue tent."

"Why that little tent?"

"Ah," he started, "because, like you, it's little and petite."

Emphasising the fact that I was considerably more vertically challenged than he, he tapped me on the head again.

Grimly, I imagined the claustrophobia, before weighing up the more pleasing prospects of having a nice, cosy place to myself.

"Not really!" he laughed. "You'll be sharing with the rest of the girls!"

Several girls and several female staff would be packed into one tent which, although large in its dimensions, would be smaller inside due to its excess of bodies.

As night rose and the sun fell behind the gleam of the bus, the square tent, used as a sort of canvas common room, filled with people. Shaun, having brought his guitar, entertained a karaoke crowd. Together, the Quartet sang *Wig Wham Bam* to great applause. Elena, cowering in the corner, was pushed to sing *Milk Has Got a Lotta Bottle*. For the encore, the superstar guitarist launched into his beloved *Needles and Pins*.

As the singing drew to a close, the radio was dragged from the bus. Muzzily, it played a repeated selection of hits from Atlantic 252. Emerging from the tent used as a kitchen, Uncle Derek and Marie produced thick rounds of toast and butter. Although hungry to the point of delirium, I declined the offer, gnawing on my lip with self-control.

— SEVENTEEN —

FERNOAKE COLLEGE OFFERED us sanctuary as the last traces of an Indian Summer met their death. Brown leaves, kicked through the playground, hitting the windows like flightless birds. Outside, young children chased one another over swings and roundabouts. Sebastian, grinning with youthful delight, enjoyed his new role as scarecrow. Seated in a damp patch of mottled mud and deceased foliage, he rocked, rhythmically, from side to side. The youngsters filled his clothes with dead leaves. With a smile from both sides, he was hoisted into a wheelbarrow by a foursome before being whirled around in a clearing of sawdust.

Turning back around to face the classroom, I heard Sally complain that her face was hot. Wrenching open the window, Vince reassured her that the cool autumn air would make her feel better.

Inside, having nothing to do, I found myself scrawling her portrait onto a scrap of lined paper.

"Written anything yet?" asked Vince, sighing.

"I wrote a detective story," I offered, "but Stacey decided to ban it. You see, it was about a singer named Saffron who was the chief suspect connected with the murder of her stage manager. Everyone knew it was too obvious for her to have been the killer, so detective Nick Rose is called in…"

"Er, Saffron isn't based on Sally, perchance?" he quizzed me.

"Sort of, but not really," I replied, hiding my face behind the doodle. "You see she's a pop star, of the old-fashioned easy-listening type, but also an actress. This character is very, *very* competitive."

"I see…"

"And the body of her co-star is found in a disused swimming pool. He was a rock star-cum-actor named Shane Dean Rossdale…"

"Not based on your dear friend, Shaun Rogers, perchance?"

"Okay, okay, okay, so he was. A little bit. You see, I wanted to honour my friends by immortalising them as characters in my story."

"And that got you in trouble with Stacey?"

"Yeah. She's a philistine! She made me put my story in the drawer and write a nice poem about 'friendship' instead."

"Original," he yawned.

"Yeah, friendship, bloody friendship! Nobody's friends here, and if you are friends, then you get split up: just like the Deadly Quartet."

"We all know why the Quartet get split up…"

"Because we're friends: *real* friends, not happy clappers who run around saying 'Good-morning-please-thank-you-would-you-like-a-nice-cup-of-tea-cringe-cringe'. We say what we mean and we mean what we say."

"Yeah," agreed Vince from behind his spectacles. "I suppose so."

"Anyway," I continued, "in this story, Nick Rose – ace detective, who I never stated was either a man *or* a woman, just to make things doubly confusing – has to put together this whole jigsaw puzzle. She finds out that Sally's best friend, but secret rival, Kirren Wren, has been sleeping with her co-star, James Taylor."

"Not based on John Taylor, was he?"

"Sceptic! Anyway, Kirren has been jealous of Sally for a long, long time. This is because, not only is Sally, sorry, I mean *Saffron*, more famous, but she is not as talented as Kirren. Kirren also has a drugs habit, originally taken up in solace to all those bad B-movie roles she gets thrown at her."

"So she's stuck playing a coke-addicted tree is she?"

"And because of this," I continued, "she goes out of her mind and goes crazy in the arms of James Taylor on the set of the latest film: *Diamond Nights*. As they are up to no good, Saffron walks in, swearing revenge."

"So get to the point! Get to the point!" urged Vince, growing weary. "Who's the killer, then?"

"Guess. It's a detective story!"

"The victim? Suicide?"

"Right! Way off! Who *doesn't* die? Who *might* be the killer? Pretend you're Nick Rose for a minute."

"Hello," he said flatly, "I'm Nick Rose, transsexual detective extraordinaire."

"Good, good, and I'll be Kirren."

Picking up a retractable biro, I theatrically plunged it into my arm: "Hey baby," I drawled in pure 1970s Americana. "Gee, man, I am so looking forward to this next here per-fowa-mance."

"And it's Westwood Scrubbins prison for you, Kirren!"

"Darn!"

He had guessed the killer without even reading my handiwork.

"Kirren Wren, I hereby sentence you to half an hour looking after the kids in the playground."

I liked time with Vince. Helping him look after the young leaf-throwers would be more fun than sitting in the classroom.

Running outside, I spun the tiny form of Jordan around in a windmill. Dark eyes shining beneath his Ferrari baseball cap, he climbed on my back for "horsey-rides". Soon a queue had formed for my equestrian services. Tired from all the exercise, I joined the squabbles for a game of hide 'n' seek. Sebastian, large and obvious, hid unconvincingly behind the shed. Jordan, always the clever one, was found at last, rolled up inside the duvet inside the playhouse.

Breezing into the dining room, I seated myself at table. Across the room stood a selection of fish, chips and beans. Taking my place in line, I cut a fish portion in half, took a small ladleful of beans and six chips. Returning to table, I poured glass after glass of water. After finishing my meal, I departed to the bathroom to wash my hands.

Inside the sacred cubicle, I prayed in silence to the god that was Kieran. Kieran, tall and muscular with a long cascade of dark hair that he tied in a pony-tail, had first appeared in the drama as a human playing card in the Queen of Hearts' parade. Since the first showing of his presence, he had revealed only slight glimmers of himself, usually when aiding the children in the playground at Fernoake. With expert precision, I painted his face in my mind. His piercing blue eyes and neatly stubbled jaw created themselves onto the blank canvas of the door as I sat in meditation.

Ten minutes flitted past in the world outside. Meanwhile, I remained lost in contemplation.

"Jessica! You in there?"

"In a minute, Eva."

This absence had proved to be a solid part of my daily routine. Each lunchtime, after finishing my portion, I would choose to indulge in my own thoughts, my own fantasy world, rather than face the tiresome reality of watching others gulp their large portions of food.

"She's *doing* something in there," I heard Eva whisper to Eunice.

"I think I *know* what she's doing," muttered Eunice.

"Washing my hands!" I called, beginning to panic.

As the air rose uncomfortably from my chest, I stifled a cough before belching ungracefully.

"She's just been sick…"

"No! I haven't!"

"I think it's time you came outside," said Eunice firmly. "You've been spending a lot of time in that loo lately!"

"Sorry?" I said with innocence. "Were you waiting?"

"You know full well what we were doing!"

Emerging, pale and embarrassed, I was led back to the table.

"From now on," said Eunice, "we are going to watch you at table. And you will *stay* at table. Just like everybody else. Until everybody has stopped eating."

"But I can be trusted. I'm a sensible eater. I'm just on a diet because you said I was fat."

"You know what we mean."

Miserably that night, I undressed in a bedroom shared by five. As the others lay drowsing, oblivious, I stared at my stomach in the mirror. It was still big. My legs were reasonably slim, but my stomach hung over my pants. I looked pregnant.

Depressingly, Calista's stomach was flat. Rolling on her pillow, playing with her curls, she had moved the mirror towards herself so as to admire her own beauty from the angle at which she lay.

Returning the mirror to its original place, I slipped into my nightie. Rising from the sheets, Calista moved it back into her chosen position. Once again, I placed it central. Once again, she placed it at Calista-level. One after another, we took fighting turns over the mirror. Behind us, from the far-end bed, Wendy began to giggle.

As Calista and myself rose to do battle, Wendy began shaking and clapping her hands at the entertainment. As the squabble grew louder, each of our intentions, spite versus vanity, becoming more aroused, the noise in the bedroom bled into uproar. Freeing the mirror from the carefully manicured hands of Calista, I was pushed to the floor. Slapping me in the face with a pristine palm, she grimaced, emphasising the rather square line of her jaw. As her bare legs kicked away, I noticed that they had broadened. Returning her slap with a harder, back-handed blow, I almost knocked the curl out of her hair. Wendy, in raptures, snuggled up in my bed for a closer view. Sally began to sing an alarm.

Pushing my elbow into Calista's flat chest, I threw her to the floor. Tomorrow she would have a nice, plummy black eye to match her mascara!

"Yoooo stole my…my…mirro!" she wept, clawing at me with her nails.

"It's *mirror*, not bloody *mirro*!" I corrected her mid-fight.

Sprawled across the floor, we rolled in near-suffocation. Opening the door on Sally's song of betrayal, Eunice walked in. With force, she tore us apart. Scraps of blonde and brunette lay maimed across the carpet.

"My mirro!" howled Calista, before being tucked back into bed.

Kirren, meanwhile, was sent to Westwood Scrubbins.

– EIGHTEEN –

"ARE YOU LONESOME tonight?" asked the earnest Trevor. "Will you miss me tonight?"

"Can I go to the loo, please?"

"Now listen here, Mrs Mopp, I thought you wanted to learn the art of the keyboard."

I hated it when he called me *Mrs Mopp*. Trevor thrived from taking blows at my confidence. By delivering each none-too-subtle put-down, he claimed that he was preparing me for the hard times to come in the Big Wide World. In reality, he just had a self-aggrandising sense of humour. This, I knew. This, he denied with a twitch of the lips and a shrug of the shoulders.

Trevor Griegson, a born "musical talent", made music a close rival even to his beloved Cheryl. His car, a sleek silver-grey Saab, was a battlefield of desire. Emblazoned across the windscreen shone the stark black print of "TREVOR 'N' CHERYL", losing its strength only to the constant discord that leaked from the stereo. Through the window came the alluring view of his compact disc collection. Tapes, to Trevor, possessed none of the refining qualities of modern-day technology. Amongst the infinite pile of processed sounds were his travelling favourites, many of them shop-bought compilations. *Disco Nites* proved a regular for his journey to work, as did *Neon Motown Remixes '91* for his tiring ride home. However, the limited joys of *Pan Pipe Medley* were shared with the residents, recently transported to the musically hollow vicinity of Sternoake.

Today, lovingly clutching the Bible of all enthusiastic keyboardists, *XR20: Pops*, he was willing to educate me in the songs of Elvis

Presley. Pointing out the correct formation of "C" on the keys, he demonstrated with his famed rendition of *Are You Lonesome Tonight?*.

"Any Duran Duran songs?"

"What, what, what?"

"Duran Duran?" I repeated.

"Aaah!" he smiled, adding unnecessary tinkles and flourishes to a tune that had once resembled *Rio*.

Suddenly, as he exploited his musical virtuosity, I remembered my fading adoration of John Taylor, now wilting in contrast to the blossoming reality of Kieran. He did not love me. John Taylor had been safe. He did not love me either, he loved Amanda De Cadenet, but he was made of paper. Safe. No reality, no disappointment.

Days ago, I had tried to learn what I called *Kieran's Song*. James Rigby had tried to teach it to me on the guitar. Sadly, I could not play it very well. Mainly due to a mixture of emotion and embarrassment, my fingers flailed clumsily over the fretboard. I had given up. The song in question had been *More Than Words* by Extreme, Kieran's favourite. My efforts had come to nothing: rather like my hopes.

In trying to play the keyboard, my musical problems were of a different nature. Trevor dampened my enthusiasm, occasionally splashing my esteem with drops of shallow compliments. He explained each method as if to a child. Still misunderstanding the formation of "beats-to-the-bar" and the letters of notes on the scale, I needed to attach labels to the keys.

As my lesson was nearly completed, I found myself pondering over the lyrics I had written earlier in the bedroom. None of them seemed to fit a tune of any sort, definitely not one of Trevor's melodies. If any tune could be found, it existed only inside my head. The song was called *On My Wall*.

"She stares at the wall, paper face is all," I had sung whilst washing my hair. "She sees and she calls and it's time to fall."

"Clumsy!" I had denounced the song before throwing it in the bin by the mattress.

Kieran had a gorgeous girlfriend. Had she been ugly, it would not have hurt so much.

"Sweets for my sweet, sugar for my honey! Milk for me cow! Ribena for Sabrina!" came the chorus over Shaun's guitar.

Simon swayed with a tambourine, swinging his ever-lengthening legs over the padded chairs. Peter Samson, now tired of the keyboard, banged a drum.

Had I possessed the looks of Kylie and the musical talent of Shaun, perhaps I could have seen some success with Kieran. He was an alluring temptation, the distance seeming further to him each day. I felt like a donkey chasing a carrot, like in old cartoons. He was out of my league.

The building was unfinished and draughty. The bedroom I shared with Wendy and Calista held no privacy. Even when I had the room to myself, I could feel the presence of the workmen outside seeping through the glass. Once, when I had secretly been applying stolen make-up, I noticed I was being admired by a middle-aged man in overalls. Whispering "Kieran" under my breath, I soon stopped, turned around, and shouted "Paedophile!" through the window. The man, embarrassed, soon disappeared.

I could have given the builders a good show. At least *someone* was interested in me. Perhaps flirting would have lifted my self-esteem a little. Star material? Only in secret.

I had sung my song to myself whilst washing my hands. I spent longer and longer in the bathroom each day, often daydreaming behind the door in secret. Nobody could disturb me, unless, of course, they banged on the door. This was my own private world. I did nothing dirty, just sat and romanticised.

Reaching a peak of miserable self-defeatism, I had smashed my wrist violently against the wall. As the bruise was acknowledged by Eva, I was given a warning not to do it again.

I wrote more lyrics inside my head, later transferring them to the notebook I kept in my blue holdall. Most of the pages in my notebook had been destroyed and flushed away. I had seen some prisoners in an old film destroy notes by washing them down the toilet.

Pulling down my adored LeBons, I patted my stomach. Pregnant? Virgin! I had lost a bit more weight. I was now seven and a half stone, but I still had puppy fat, especially around my gut. However, my legs were slim. Most days I wore leggings to show off my best features. My belly remained undercover, usually swamped by a baggy T-shirt or sweater.

"Get out of that toilet!" came the voice of Eunice.

Unlocking the door, I was greeted by a scowl of suspicion.

"Downstairs!"

"I had dirt in my eye!" I lied in protest. "I was just trying to get it out."

"You are being very silly towards food!" she warned, ignoring what I had just said.

"I'm not!" I yelled, eyes smarting. "I eat everything on my plate. Remember? 'A little bit of everything?'"

"You eat what little you actually *put* on your plate," she corrected me. "From now on, we shall have to watch you closer *whenever* you're in the bathroom."

"Even when I'm in the bath?" I gasped with horror.

"Yes, if we have to. Even when you're in the bath."

"But you'll see my blubber…and my bum…and my boobs…and my *women's bits*!"

Shocked, I dropped to the floor. Wailing, I was escorted back down the stairs.

"Oh de-ar!" said Eva, sustaining each note with smug pretence. "Oh, I do think that our Jess is looking rather like a bag of bones."

"Yes," agreed Eunice on my arm, "I think she looks a little bit poorly. Look at this…"

Prodding my chest, she turned me around towards the crowd of gathering females.

"Her boobs have disappeared!"

"I've always had small boobs," I protested.

"You can't even hold your head up straight."

"We'll have to watch you in the bath!"

"I'm still a whole stone heavier than Kylie," I stated.

"If Kylie was as thin as you say she is, she would crack in the middle."

My waist was prodded.

"Get off!"

"There's a space between her thighs, isn't there, Carrie?"

"Yes, there is, isn't there, Miriam?"

"Her knees knock together."

"What's wrong with my legs?"

The physical inquisition continued around me.

"Her arms are like sparrow's legs!"

My arms had always been thin. Only my belly and face were fat.

"Exercise is better than starving yourself."

"I do the video twice a week and walk up and down the stairs ten times after each meal!"

"It's bad to exercise after meals. It makes you throw up!"

Their accusing eyes hit me in the face.

"I don't throw up! I *never* throw up!"

"But you're always in the toilets!"

"Yes, to be alone. To think!"

"And making yourself sick, no doubt!"

"Princess Diana used to do that. It's called *bulimia*!"

"I don't do bulimia! Really! I don't!"

Pulling a face, I put my fingers in my mouth: "Look! *Look!* I can't do it! I CAN'T DO IT! I CAN'T!"

"It rots your insides! Your teeth fall out and your breath smells! Just like an old woman."

"Men like girls with a bit of meat on them," added Marie, proud of her own voluptuous figure. "What men like is the Marilyn Monroe figure. She wasn't skinny."

"She's dead," I added, temporarily silencing the mob.

"You look like a little girl," said Carrie.

"At least I don't look as old as you. And I won't let you make me get fat. I'll eat what I want to. If you put fat in front of me or on my plate, I don't have to eat it. If you make me stay in until I've eaten it, when it's starting to rot, decay and go off, I still won't eat it. It's my body and I'll go on a diet if I want to."

"You'll end up in Constance Hill Hospital. Then the nurses will force-feed you."

"I'll escape," I defied them. I had a talent for escapism, a talent admired by Simon among others.

"They'll be watching over you. The nurses there will make *us* seem like Little Bo Peep."

"I'll still escape."

"Yes, you *will* get out of Constance Hill," added Carrie with wit. "You'll get so skinny you'll disappear."

"And that'll be a relief for all of us," whispered Miriam.

"I heard that!"

Beneath my jumper and beloved LeBons, I knew, in my own mind, that they were jealous. Most of them were fat and none of them had the willpower to change this, or their undesirable shapes. At mealtimes I had watched, in disgust, as they had shovelled helping after helping of dessert into their eagerly open mouths. Chips and chocolate had so often passed their lips and no food was sacred. None of them had principles. None could resist the bestial urges of hunger. All of them were suffocating within their own individual duvets of fat, swallowed whole inside their own wobbling flesh, unaware of the grotesque nature of their appearance. A few of them even struggled to climb the stairs, weighed down by the immense bulk of their bodies, immobile, clumsy and panting for breath.

Together, to hide their resentment towards their own smothered bodies, they would try to break my resolve, destroy what strength of will I possessed, fatten me up, ruin any bodily pride I possessed and convert me into one of *them*. They would destroy my threat to their own low self-esteem.

They were hypocrites: all of them! At mealtimes, a table was kept separate for those, mainly girls, on diets. As the young people suffering from weight problems were encouraged to eat less, to take fruit instead of pudding, to cut down the amounts on their plates, the staff would carefully keep watch, scrutinising each bite. Then later, in the staff room, they would gorge themselves on crisps and chocolate bars, luxuries forbidden to us in the diet group. Sometimes Uncle Derek would rouse the male young people into taking second helpings larger than their first amounts, proclaiming the lucky eaters were "young growing lads". Whilst a lad was "strapping" or "hearty", a lass would be disregarded as "tubby" or "needs to lose a few pounds".

Before the start of my diet, I had often taken second helpings on purpose. This was to prove that a lass, as well as a lad, could indulge: an early bit of feminism on my part. Usually, this indulgence had been looked upon with sour eyes and warnings of "It'll lead to obesity!". Without relenting, although flinching inside, I had continued to take action, biting eagerly into my second helping of apple crumble.

Inevitably, as each helping of rebellion had been devoured, the weight had begun to grow and then consume the shape of my body. Unhappy at eight and a half stone, I had decided to lose weight. After successfully losing the excess mass, I was now being punished for my efforts.

Whatever I gained was criticised. Whatever I lost was criticised. My body and eating habits, constantly under scrutiny, would always be wrong.

I was thinner than Calista. Although not as classically pretty or easy on the lenses of cameras, I was an entire stone lighter than her. The former object of my intense jealousy was now filling out, destroying her superior status somewhat. Even her curls were going. Her long, blonde tresses, once tumbling with girlish glamour over her shoulders, had now been restricted to an untidy bob, rumoured to have been cut by her mother. Instead of ringlets, she now had a straight crown and frizzy ends. Her appeal had dwindled slightly. The constant application of make-up had grown less, the flaunting of frocks had near ceased and comparisons to top models and film stars had grown less. When curling tongs were aimed at her hair, she flinched. When a mascara wand was offered to transform her lashes into never-ending prongs of indigo allure, she pushed it away. Her scribblings had stopped. There was no more mention of golden hair or curls.

As the inquisition departed whispering snatches about Belsen and Cambodia, I returned to my seat in the common room. Break was almost over. Sighing, I hid my face behind a magazine. Deacon, seated next to me, gave me a hug. Together, we were Miss World and Mr Universe.

Stretching his muscular arm around my shoulders, he was discouraged, by Trevor, for "inappropriate behaviour".

Deacon's hair had grown long since the move, scraping the edges of his rugby shirt collar. His fringe, jovially cut by Trevor in a moment of mirth, hit his forehead like a chestnut razor blade. Unaware of such a hirsute disfigurement, Deacon wondered little at the laughter of his peers.

"I'm safe," I sighed with gratitude. "I've got Duvetman to protect me."

Suddenly it occurred to me that I was the Big Girl here. Despite being physically smaller than I had been, I was the Leader of the Girl's Landing, Queen of the Bathrooms. Shuddering at the thought, I vowed to stand against bathroom investigation: not just for myself, but for all the non-verbals, twiddlers and bangers of the girls' dormitories.

Elena, Sabrina and now Calista were constantly scrutinised in the bath. Calls of "She's getting big thighs" and "She needs a bigger bra" were often followed by howls of amusement from behind the door.

Striding over towards the watchful presence of Eva, I confronted her with the question: "Why do you watch us in the bathrooms?"

Her reply: "Because it's our job to do so."

"When you go home," I continued, "do you have people watching *you* in the bath?"

"Only my husband."

"Why do you watch Elena?"

"Because she bites herself."

"What if she *wants* to bite herself?"

"We don't let her. It doesn't look good."

"What if she *needs* to bite herself?"

"Nobody *needs* to bite themselves."

"Then why do you watch Sabrina? She never bites herself."

"Because she flaps. She rocks and twiddles. It's our job to stop her."

"But why do you stare at her boobs?"

"It's none of your business! Go and sit down!"

Re-seated, I felt the heat rise under my collar. Elena marched backwards and forwards from wall to wall, touching her breasts as she went.

Deacon licked the floor.

"Tonight we'll be watching *you* in the bathroom too," stated Eva before adopting a tone of regret. "You used to be the *sensible* one."

"The boring one," I sighed.

Boring and *sensible* always meant the same thing, rather like *responsible.*

"Oh dear," sighed Eva. "We thought you were doing oh so well. You'd got so close to earning our trust...and now we know that you just don't want to grow up."

"I'm fifteen. I've just had my birthday."

"I think that tonight you can stay in and do art and craft instead of going on the cinema trip."

Normally, I would have been upset by this, but the cinema trip involved a kiddies Disney adventure. Art and craft, however, was a different matter. Instead of the expected images of painting and pottery, the activities involved making innumerable greetings cards from dried flowers. As there was a seasonal theme, we would sometimes mass produce an endless supply of Christmas garlands. Usually, I would finish the session with sticky fingers, glue beneath my nails and numerous paper-cuts for my efforts. Needless to say, I had found a way to make money.

Normally a dull slog accompanied by the chosen music of Uncle Derek, or Trevor, fast becoming a junior version of his mentor, I had asked if I could make origami baubles to sell. Surprisingly, I had been allowed. After selling off the last supply, I almost had enough money to buy presents for my family and friends. I had gained satisfaction as each metallic bloom appeared between my hands, that many Christmas trees would be blossoming with my creations.

Today, as a lesson for my immaturity, I would be given the tedious task of cutting up the tissue paper for streamers.

Sitting at the table in the back room, knowing that today was not a money-maker, I reluctantly picked up the scissors. I felt like dragging them across my wrist. Gloomily, I leant down on my elbows, staring heartlessly at the mounds of paper.

Droning speakers muffled songs of good cheer and advertisements for turkey and Christmas pudding. I would not be eating any. Thankfully, Simon had stolen Trevor's *Christmas Disco Classics*.

As the small crowd ceased in their artful folding and glueing, another announcement came on the radio: Freddie Mercury had died.

— NINETEEN —

"BUDDY YOU'RE A BOY MAKIN' BIG NOISE PLAYIN' IN THE STREET GONNA BE A BIG MAN SOME DAY!"

Together, in cacophonous unison, the Quartet was invincible. Shaun and Simon hollered and yelled whilst Peter Samson screamed through a homemade megaphone. Standing atop the horizontal ladder, I gymnastically stomped along its quivering bars, looking down at the twelve-foot drop beneath me, unafraid. Ignoring a warning gesture from Trevor, I leapt down onto my haunches before straddling the bars. The four of us were unstoppable.

"WE WILL! WE WILL! ROCK YOU!" *Bang-bang! Crunch! Bang-bang! Crunch!*

"This one's for Freddie!"

Shuddering with the rhythm of many feet, the wooden fortress lived, breathing and panting with each word we sang. Threatening to crumble beneath each foot-stamp, or fold with each hand-clap, it felt its bones pounded into the wood-chippings. As the timber rumbled beneath the feet of the growing congregation, the singing increased into uproarious tones.

"WE WILL! WE WILL! ROCK YOU! ROCK YOU! ROCK YOU!"

Launching into a frenzied solo on his air guitar, Shaun was held as an idol. Teenagers and youngsters alike threw themselves at his feet. Running with Simon down the slanting aisle, we reached Neil, hiding underground. Rocking the wall, we encouraged him to join us.

"Now! Give a warm welcome to…NEIL PROSHKA!" I cried, bringing him up for air. "And also joining us for this live concerto is the

loving wife and concubine of Shaun Everett Rogers: MISS…
DIODE…CAPACITATOR!"

Miss Diode Capacitator, electrical whizz, was, in true name, Anita
Dawes, last remembered as the *Voice of Lewis Carroll*. Anita, a tall,
slender blonde with a badly-cut bob and even worse-cut leggings, was
Shaun's partner in the carnal sense. The Bonnie to his Clyde, she was a
menace in the swimming pool and an honorary member of the
Quartet. A resident of Fernoake, she came daily to study electronics in
the art and technology section. At present, she was building her own
radio. Often, knowing how inept I was at all things technical, she
would aid me in building my own.

I had brought Shaun and Anita together through a series of intro-
ductions. Now together, they would roll amongst the wood-chippings
within the nurturing walls of the fortress, rubbing the splinters from
one-another's backs.

"WE WILL! WE WILL! ROCK YOU!"

Orders falling unheard and unlistened to, Trevor waved his arms in
the air as if trying to grasp a hold of whatever little control he held.

"Ignore that daft old policeman!" she nudged before raising the
singing even higher.

"Siege! Riot!" yelled Simon, laughing and swinging his increasing
lankiness towards us.

"Did you know that I'm a vampire?" whispered Anita, pulling me
into the underground hideaway.

"A vampire?"

"Yeah. I'm a vampire, a real vampire, from the planet Vampire," she
said, biting me on the neck. "I'm also a villain!"

"I've already bit Shaun," she grinned. "We'll be spending eternity
together."

"But he'll be dead in a fortnight. Sorry, *leaving* in a fortnight," I
sighed, knowing that even the undead must leave Sternoake.

"He'll always be in my heart," she said wistfully. "His blood pumps
around and around my vampire heart."

Calista, sulky and morose, sat sheltered beneath the slide, blocking
her ears to the din.

"C'mon, Jess!" enthused Anita. "Let's make Calista bald! I know all about acid. In fact, I sweat acid. *See?*"

Holding up her hand, globules of sweat glowed in the sunlight. Anita, possibly due to her hyperactivity, had permanently sweaty palms.

"See this acid on my hands? It can't hurt you or Shaun, because you're both vampires! But it can burn humans!"

Skulking with menace towards the cringing form of Calista, she wiped her palms across the girl's face, smudging whatever little make-up she now wore.

"Hah! Burn! You are the policeman's spy! Yes, you are one of *them*, the Vampire Police! You'll never hunt us down! You are a VP! But we are vampires! Together, we acid-palmed bloodsuckers can never be defeated!"

"Oh shit!" I nudged as Anita stood looming. "Here comes Trevor, *in person*, we'd better take cover for a while!"

"Burn, VP, burn!" she called with spite, before disappearing with me under the timber roof.

"It's dark. He'll never see us!"

"I like the dark," whispered Anita, giggling. "The dark is our friend, our *best* friend."

Together, we scratched our symbols into the dust before scrambling back into the light to aid the ongoing riot.

"WE WILL! WE WILL! ROCK YOU!"

"DOWN WITH THE VAMPIRE POLICE! DOWN WITH VPs! DOWN WITH VPs!"

Above our heads, Simon began showering the staff with wood-chippings. Trevor, clearly unamused, called up more force in his frustration. Eva and Stacey appeared from the playing field. Threatened by warnings from every corner, we continued to grow yet more invincible.

"Stacey!" moaned Trevor. "These juveniles are behaving in a most inappropriate manner."

"Ah! Speaketh Mister Thesaurus," I murmured to Anita, who was suffocating with her own hysteria.

Gareth sat, singing along with his new twiddle: a toy guitar. His piano had died along with its batteries. Seizing it from his hands, Anita handed it, lovingly, to Shaun. Refusing it, through slight embarrassment, Shaun passed it to the revelling Simon who held it proudly aloft like a trophy. Approaching, Trevor's pear-shaped head now resembled a throbbing beetroot, fresh from the pickle jar. Simon, like a bull on the charge, aimed his vitriol at this flailing beacon.

"WE WILL! WE WILL! ROCK YOU! Lallall Trevor comin' to stop our bonny yusik! HA!"

"Simon Hirst!" bellowed the angry VP. "If you don't stop this nonsense now, you can sit inside and do me some lines!"

"No silly lallall lines for me, our lallall Trevor with the big, red siren! That Peter Samson can do lines while I play on castle!"

"Simon Hirst! You've just lost all your chances! Come down imme-diately!"

"Not comin' down!" he cried defiantly. "Bonny Uncle Derek and bonny Damon would let me play on castle! I'll set bonny Damon on you! 'E'll sort you out, 'e will!"

Impulsively, the toy guitar threw itself from Simon's hands, hitting his tormentor on the temple.

Shocked at his own actions, Simon fled to the safety of Shaun and myself.

"Don't let 'im get me!" he cried, almost in tears. "Let 'im get that Peter Samson instead."

As reinforcements returned from the coffee break, the riot was quashed. Shaun was given a warning, Simon a seat behind the wall and a sheet of lines whilst Peter Samson was mainly ignored. Anita and I were subjected to a long discussion on responsible behaviour. Later in the day, we sneaked into the back common room to play on Trevor's latest toy.

It was an organ, not unlike a Hammond, and monstrous in size. Some of its keys were missing and its variety of sound settings ranged from groan to rumble. Together, we could create our own grotesque melodic prodigies to the delight of our willing audience. Our favourite was a funereal dirge that would not have been out of place in an early Hammer movie. As Shaun played out his death march, Anita bared her fangs.

To the beat of the bossa nova rhythm, we would pick up the pool cues for a sport that resembled snooker merged with fencing. Occa-sionally, a ball would hit Shaun on the lap. Simon was keen to drop the eight ball from the window like a bomb, just in case Trevor dared pass below. When the organ lost its appeal, I would bring down *We Will Rock You* to play on the stereo, which was, by now, a clapped-out box of loose fuses.

Elena, now neglected by the affections of Shaun, would sit, calling his name under the watchful glare of Sybil. As every stitch was dropped into her ongoing tapestry, she would sigh over his last touch. Perhaps she was envying Anita. Once, desperately needing her regular tickle from him, she had called me by his name, hoping I would do the same. As I obliged, I imagined Elena pictured his face above my hands.

Shaun now had an immense following among the female young people. Elena, his first love now waning, had to compete with the newly lit Catherine wheel that was Anita. My own love for him, although platonic, had become like the flesh bond of a Siamese twin. We now thought almost alike, sharing words almost psychically. We had our own language. Despite this, I was hardly jealous of his new relationships with women.

Added to his harem was Wendy, releasing the strength of her devotion by squeezing his legs whenever he sat down. She would whisper sweet everythings into his ear whilst it was too busy listening to various Bond themes. She would become hysterical and hug him. He would become slightly embarrassed and move on to another of his, less passionate, concubines.

The new arrival to Sternoake, Rhiona McEwan, was also a big fan of our leader. Scottish by birth and barely thirteen years old, she was short and podgy with a shock of curly hair. Her full lips dropped chatter like pinballs and her green eyes would sparkle at him whenever he came near. Usually if Shaun was occupied, she would cling heavily to my arm, laughing and repeating to herself over his charms.

Many times she had joined the growing numbers on the fortress, enjoying the sheer noise and repetition of our revelry. Sometimes, in her honour, we would add a few Madonna songs to the regular Queen selection.

Madonna was Rhiona's other idol, second only to Shaun. On a good day, if she had controlled her temper and outbursts of emotional frenzy, she would be allowed into my room for a Madonna make-up session. Using an old red lipstick, a hardly-used Boots make-up set and an eyeliner pen, I could transform the face before me into the visage of the pointy-breasted superstar.

Rhiona had a terrible swearing habit, far worse than my own. The odd "Fuck you!" would result in a grounding or the cancellation of all Madonna-related activities. This swearing, she insisted, was involuntary. A former resident of other sorts of care, she was familiar with

Tourette's syndrome. If she was ever caught repeatedly saying the F-word, or even, when she was infuriated, the C-word, she would convince the displeased member of staff that she was suffering from Tourette's. Sometimes she would even mimic the tics.

As a bond formed between Rhiona and myself, we became both the best of friends and the worst of enemies. Needing affection, yet craving confrontation, Rhiona made me her partner in Madonna-ness, but also the wicked witch. Pictures appeared of witches around the common room. Drawn by the hand of my venomous pal, I noticed something familiar about the pictures. "They're of Jessica!" she would scream with pride. A few times, I had held her in an argument over such matters. This, she had enjoyed more than even the witch-hunt itself. Once when I had offered to help her shave her legs in the bathroom, I had been showered with talcum powder and thrown into the bath. Rhiona, laughing, had thrown a punch at my chest. Raising my hands in self-defence, I had thrown her to the floor. Upon hearing the uproar, Eunice had stood me in the corner for disruptive behaviour, giving Rhiona a mere warning. Before vowing revenge, I realised that Rhiona would enjoy such a challenge.

Rhiona liked to fight with everyone. When she won, she would cause the young person or staff member to crack through all restraints. Finding herself homesick at Sternoake, she had picked up a pen during a session of writing lines. Instead of writing on the page, she had emblazoned the wall with the legend "SCOTLAND THE BRAVE!".

As various loving "Fuck yous" appeared over the furniture, it seemed that Rhiona's Tourette's spilled over into the written word. Her face could be seen grinning with malice over every profanity she scrawled. She would stutter the words as she created her art, often in a loud voice. Trevor had threatened to remedy this with a gag.

Fixing herself with mental glue to her beloved Shaun, she added his stammer to her own speech, even imitating the endless pauses he could leave between sentences. An incredible mimic, she learnt the traits of Simon's dialect, sometimes replacing her thick Scottish accent with his Yorkshire one. Nobody was immune to her impersonations. Everybody lost a part of themselves in her routines. She could be both a great source of comedy and a great source of irritation. To Rhiona, being the latter gave her the greater thrill.

Behind the fortress, across the uneven playing field, stood the dark thatch of trees, weeds and empty crisp packets that formed our forest. This untamed woodland provided the ideal hiding place for any young person wishing to avoid the glare of the staff. Naturally, it became the favourite haunt of Shaun and his harem. One by one and blushing, his partners would emerge. It was unlikely that Shaun ever went all the way, but nevertheless his lovers appeared satisfied.

Simon loved the forest for reasons of his own. He would collect things from the undergrowth, like old batteries and car parts, and hide them in his secret spot. Some of his stolen tapes later joined them. His nickname, *Robin Hood Junior*, suited him. Peter Samson, recently having watched Kevin Costner's *Robin Hood*, would mutter lines of dialogue from the film whilst kicking leaves about with verve. Jonathan would wander over to clear them up.

Calista, never far from the eyes of her protectors, preferred to sit on a bench and watch the players play. Rarely did she kick a football or handle a cricket bat. Instead she preferred to anxiously soak up what little sun she could find.

From behind, it was now impossible to tell what gender she might be. Her hair, now cropped short due to years of styling abuse, stuck out from her head in uneven tufts. Refusing to brush it, or even allow others to handle the task, she would prevent its growth by pulling out handfuls in the bathroom. On seeing her in action, I had held out a comb in the hope it would inspire guilt. This had merely encouraged her further.

When she stood up, however, her gender was obviously of the female type. Instead of dieting, which she had always been meticulous about, she now helped herself to chips and fry-ups. When she went home for the holidays, her mum would feed her chocolate to "cheer her up". This was not surprising as her mouth now refused to smile her, once beaming, glitter grin. Instead it remained fixed in a thin-lipped scowl. As a result of this gorging, she had widened at the hips and thighs considerably, her chest remaining small and boyish.

Her face was no longer painted with lipstick and rouge and her skin was dry. The only words she now spoke or wrote were simple requests for a drink or puzzle. Conversation was beneath even hair-brushing on her list of priorities.

In her constant need to avoid the attention of those who fussed over her, Calista had destroyed all her dresses at home. If the rumours were true, she had cut them up with pinking shears. The one that had survived was worn with reluctance. No tops could be worn unless they had a collar. Rugby shirts were her favourite. If no collar existed, then the shirt would be torn at the seams.

Walking past Calista with my long hair plaited behind me, I held the football in my hands. Deacon jogged beside me whilst Rhiona begged me for a Madonna session. Suddenly, I looked across towards the figure on the bench and felt a prickle of guilt. Once, I had been Calista's underdog rival for the bathroom and mirror, not to mention the attentions of the staff. I had won this battle and, undeniably, played a part in her downfall. Part of me suddenly felt bad. I felt like a shiny-surfaced apple that, once picked from the tree, was, literally, rotten to the core.

Beneath my smile, I was definitely no picture of perfection. I had gained weight again and had called Calista "beefy" in attempts to shift the weight problem. I was worse than the staff. Later, I had smashed myself on the leg with a cricket bat to kill off the fat before it grew back like a fungus.

A song had been written in Calista's honour. To the tune of *Walking in the Air*, we would sing: "Ca-lista's got no hair! Her bonce is very bare…to-daaay!"

Strangely, Eva had encouraged me with such mocking comedy. Now others sang the song with me. Even Peter Samson sang it when prompted.

"Ca-lista's got no hair!" sang Eva and Rhiona into the acid face of their target.

Like a bald Delilah in Samson's oversized shoes, she had lost all self-worth. Her few words gradually became just murmurs or an agitated guttural stammer. She lost her temper more. Often she was lost *inside* her temper. Nobody could talk her out of her newly adopted ways.

"And I remember when our Calista used to look like a top model!" regretted Eva across the table, the malice in her voice becoming almost high camp.

Blank-eyed and speechless, Calista gazed at the carpet.

"And I remember when she were a right proper little chatterbox!"

Straightening out her collar, Calista took her empty plate and placed it, silently, on the hatch.

— TWENTY —

"THE LATE SHAUN Everett Rogers," I practised saying beneath hushed breath. "The late Shaun Everett Rogers."

Slowly drifting on the shadows of its tyres, a black Ford Escort pulled up into the driveway. Shining black metal blinded the eyes of the small crowd in its way. Shaun, surprisingly light in his gait, walked casually away from his farewells. Simon, near tearful, removed his baseball cap in honour of the departed.

"Don't phone me," he said with deliberately wooden thespian skill. "I'll put the phone down."

A shared sigh ran through the sombre group.

He continued, noble and presidential, our leader: "Don't write to me. I'll rip up the letter. You're not going to see me any more, and I'm not going to see you."

Hurt shot through the ventricles of my heart as I felt my mentor slipping away.

"This place holds nothing but bad memories. Now I am gone, you too will be gone to me. I would like you to remember that I am dead."

He paused after dropping the word "dead".

A silence followed. Shaun climbed into the hearse without waving and was escorted to pastures new.

Slowly and mournfully, the day died with Shaun. Rhiona, forever asking questions, demanded the whereabouts of her lost lover. Simon became withdrawn and uncharacteristically melancholic.

Inside myself, I knew that the inevitable had happened. After all, Shaun was twenty, two years older than most elderly young people. Inside, I knew the reality could not be fought, but inside I lamented my brother in thought, my platonic soulmate, my mentor. If not my hero, he was at least the greatest influence on me at Sternoake. He was gone. Dead.

After his passing, Elena called me "Shaun" more than ever. Rhiona even took up the habit herself. Our Siamese bond could not be broken by distance. He was still a part of me, living on in my methods, my mannerisms, my humour. Shaun had left his mark. Shaun was still at Sternoake.

I never received any trace of his address, not even a phone number. Eventually, I accepted his "death".

Following that dry day on the March concrete, I would fool myself that he was still around. A snatch of a tattered blue dressing gown would flicker down the corridor; the covers of an old book would be found, discarded, behind the bookcase; his voice, recorded from French lessons, would be played back from a tape recorder. These were all traces of his ghost.

The *Late* Shaun Everett Rogers. Rhiona still scrawled his name across her geography book. Some residents even spoke his name from the quiet room, as though in prayer. We whispered in our hushed groups about his return. His face still appeared in my artwork, sometimes unintentionally. He was the patron saint of all wrongdoers.

"Leave off, our lallall Bill!" Simon would cry when in jeopardy. "I'll set that Shaun Rogers onto you! 'E'll come BACK and sort you out for good!"

His return would be like the Second Coming at Sternoake.

As Simon solemnly tuned the radio to the local station, the song that played was bizarrely appropriate. It was Blue Oyster Cult's *Don't Fear the Reaper*. Turning towards the single working speaker, his ruddy features paled in remembrance.

Shaun had played that song on his guitar during the camping holiday. As ever, he had used the basis of the song to create drug metaphors. Listening to the strumming of the guitar, he likened each note of music to a drop of heroin. Simon, unaware of what heroin was, had enjoyed the idea of a magic liquid that made you smile.

Obsessions and drugs had a lot in common. A junkie was addicted to heroin or cocaine, Shaun to music. He was a music junkie: old B-sides being his class A fix. Both obsessions and drugs could create a feeling of warmth, a sense of security and fulfilment. Both could lead to loss, denial and a paranoid sense of something, somehow being incomplete. Obsessions could provide a temporary fix: that lost cassette filling a gap, but soon a new addition to the collection would be needed. Obsessions pushed the individual further, but never far enough.

The obsession was a benevolent tyrant: it caused happiness, but needed *more*. It could blind the host with compulsions, creating mental blinkers. The obsessive was a racehorse sprinting towards the finish line, but the line kept being moved further and further away.

The obsession could drain thought from other channels of the mind, sucking it towards its own individual cause. The obsession could be a parasite. Fed until glutted, it needed more mental and material food to bloat itself more.

Music was a fun obsession, but other obsessions could be less enjoyable. These compulsions became traps, as had my obsession with germs. Now I had a new obsession.

My jeans were creased. Looking down, I felt the master take hold. I *became* my obsession. I *became* the need to iron out that crease, to obliterate the enemy. That tiny enemy, that small fold of material, had taken over, creating its own warped logic. That logic told me that with that crease in my jeans, my appearance would be laughable. To leave the crease alone would be unbearable. I would rush to my room to iron it out. The iron was cumbersome, the board heavy and difficult to carry upstairs, but the voice kept calling me. At a point, I was near-deranged by the intruder on my jeans and imagined the worst. Perhaps I might accidentally burn my arm on the hot iron? It did not matter as long as the crease was gone. The crease must go! There must be NO creases on my jeans, just a smooth, unrippled sea of denim, free of any such disfigurements.

Almost tripping over the wire, I tore off my garments, laying them flat across the ironing board. As steam threw itself from the spout, I felt myself wanting to punish that crease, to make it suffer before its imminent demise.

Suddenly, as I was standing half-naked, the push of a door interrupted my efforts. Standing, hands on hips, Eunice forced her face into a frown of disapproval.

"Those jeans were ironed this morning!"

Alarmed, I replied: "The staff didn't iron them properly. I had to iron them myself."

"So why are you ironing them again?"

"Because the staff didn't iron them properly. There's a crease."

"Look at that!" urged Eunice, holding up the jeans that had raised my anxiety levels to boiling point. "That *crease*, as you call it, is so small it's unnoticeable."

"But *I* noticed it."

"I think you should put your jeans on, and put the ironing board away," said Eunice, thinly disguising a command as a suggestion.

"You shouldn't be in my room," I retorted, continuing to iron.

Eunice continued to challenge me, despite the hot iron. She gave the threat, pretending it was an option: "If you really want to do some ironing, you can do the laundry sheets as well."

"No," I said, adding a full stop.

"Well then, put the ironing board away and stop imagining things!"

Eunice, like many staff, had divided her personality between enforcer and friend. This duality cut a thick line between Eunice The Staff Member and Eunice The Pal. Eunice The Pal was more fun. Eunice The Pal owned two small dogs named Kizzy and Kelly, loved to sing along to Queen in the minibus and liked to open the windows to spread the music across the countryside. This Eunice delighted in the affections of Deacon, accepted jokes on the part of her gingerness and was a rival to Marie and me at football. Eunice The Staff Member was more difficult. Eunice The Staff Member followed rules and made sure that all the young people displayed good conduct and carried out their domestic duties. Eunice The Staff Member was a slave to rules as much as I was a slave to my obsessions.

Other staff members were obsessed with rules, and to a much greater degree than Eunice. Bill still insisted that all young people eat "a little bit of everything" at mealtimes and kept a watchful eye on those who needed to be punished for not doing so. The rule book was *his* Bible, as the *Chronicle* had been Shaun's. Like the Bible, the rule book could be twisted to meet the needs of the one who read it. Bill would lay down the law onto the young people, but often break it himself. Once I had witnessed him taking extra chocolate biscuits from the cupboard, leaving none in reserve. When I asked him if the biscuits were for the young people, he had replied: "No. They're just for staff." As the staff ate their treats in front of the empty-mouthed young people, I had questioned if this was right. He had just replied: "I'm in charge and you're not."

Bill loved discipline, if it was *his* discipline. Handing out the punishments, he got pleasure from such a sense of power. The smallest offence, such as talking in the middle of somebody else's sentence, could become a crime. If Bill was in charge and if Bill was having a bad day, then *anything* could earn a sheet of lines or a stint in the quiet room.

Addicted to power, Bill was also addicted to cigarettes. Shaun and I had spun our wit over his compulsive smoking habit. The very thought of a fag would send Bill's lungs into rapture. Nicotine was a drug and Bill was a junkie.

Ironically, young people, even if over the age of eighteen, were banned from smoking. We were also banned from alcohol and, naturally, drugs. Our solvent sniffing gave us a release. None of us were addicted to it. If anything, the thrill of defying authority and hiding out in the loft was greater than the buzz from the solvents themselves.

Shaun had displayed power as great as Bill's. Bill enforced where Shaun rebelled. Shaun had no privileges and no authority, but he was popular and influential among the young people. If Bill was the chief of police, then Shaun had been a sort of Aspergic Godfather. We had been his gang, he had been our leader.

Once, on a rare visit to the staff room, I had been baffled by the amount of obsessive card playing. The staff had to get each card exactly right: the right place, the right time, the right motion. Others filled in pools coupons with logic furrowed across their brows. A few played hand-held computer games, paying incredible attention to their own accuracy. I wondered, perhaps, if the staff had Asperger's syndrome. Maybe they hid it in order to work at Sternoake. The thought stayed with me for a while, then left looking over its shoulder.

Wayne, alias Fat Freddie Mercury, would often request Simon's Gameboy to play on. Simon, seeing Wayne as a friend, was unaware of such cupboard love. The Gameboy would be loaned until its batteries ran dry. Luckily, Anita knew how to recharge its power.

Super Mario Bros was Simon's favourite game. Returning from the holidays with a downy moustache (later shaved off by Uncle Derek) and a red baseball cap, he looked every inch a taller version of his simulated hero.

Tetris was my own personal favourite. You had to catch falling blocks and arrange them to make horizontal lines. Wayne, on not catching a block accurately, had declared the game "Autistic!". The game was focused on structure and regularity. Naturally, many autistic people excelled at it, Peter Samson being champion.

Ironically, I had none of the usual logic-based gifts bestowed on those with Asperger's and autism. I found reading a map impossible and the video remote an enigma. Despite this, I came third in the Tetris league.

As Anita and Neil excelled at all things technological, I would prefer to sit in a classroom with a book. Although conventionally seen as being far removed from the logic-based nature of technology, I found that literature had its own structures and logistical aspects. Perhaps it was my Asperger's that had helped me obsessively learn sentence-structure and grammar. My spelling was usually impeccable, but if a word I could spell had never been spoken before me, often I could pronounce it wrong.

Some young people could read, but not put sentences together. A few of them would sit reading catalogues or telephone directories for pleasure. They would read quietly then shout out the words they recognised.

My own reading consisted mainly of lucky finds from car boot sales. I would often visit these with Dad. As a meticulous collector of teen pop annuals, I would come across dog-eared *Look Ins* with Hitler 'taches scrawled across faces and the crossword filled in with purple biro. I would chance upon pristine copies of *Blue Jeans* and *My Guy* from the seventies and eighties. After hoarding over thirty of these in my collection, I had a technicolour library of nostalgia at my command. Sometimes, on being transported to modern times past, I would believe that my life would have been happier had I been fifteen in 1976. I would have been a glam rocker or a punk, or, better still, a devotee of the fresh-faced blondness that was Roger Taylor.

Roger had won the battle of the Taylors against John. Although now middle-aged, portly and balding, I saw him as a slim twenty-six-year-old, sounding the gong, bare-chested, at the climax of *Bohemian Rhapsody*. I loved it when he wrote his own songs and sang his own vocals on Queen's albums. His voice was husky, desperate sounding, if a little high-pitched.

My love also brought devastation. Married to Debbie Leng, some twenty years his junior, their image together would cause me to lapse into obsessive despair. She had been the tall, skinny, blonde Flake Girl, the Flake Girl who nibbled chocolate yet never grew fat. Like the twins of any obsession, my fixation with my beloved Roger brought me satisfaction and dissatisfaction, joy and desperation.

It was not only pop annuals that I read, but horror stories. I would find worn copies of *The Pan Book of Horror Stories* in many an Oxfam shop. Usually these stayed hidden under my mattress or locked in my bedroom at home. This was because many staff thought they contained "offensive subject matter". These books were both cathartic and addictive to my bored teenage mind. I had written my own stories in the horror genre, basing the hero/victim character on Shaun. He was the only person other than myself that was ever allowed to read such bizarre creations.

On picking up *Wuthering Heights* in the classroom, I had started the first chapter out of curiosity. I had heard the song by Kate Bush and wondered how it related. Jan, the English teacher, had encouraged me to read it in its entirety. Predictably, I had seen myself as Cathy and Kieran as Heathcliff. My mind was always full of comparisons.

Once, on a warm, sunny break, I had watched the others play outside in the garden. I had not been grounded, I was merely deep in constructing a piece entitled *A Day in the Life of a T-Shirt*. On marking the final, if epic, result, with its mention of humans as giants and the wardrobe as a fortress, Jan had added the unforgettable comment in the margin: "What pub had you been to before you wrote this?"

– TWENTY-ONE –

ALTHOUGH MARRIED AND a parent to three children, my mother was never short of admirers at the young offenders prison at which she taught art. A dark-haired, slim woman with large brown eyes that seemed to rule her face, she would observe each piece of art brought before her, contemplating her own career, on the side, as a freelance painter. Often she would recreate Durham Cathedral, amongst other elegant ancients, in meticulous detail. Added to her portfolio were images of country gardens, garnished usually with a single, slightly malevolent looking, Siamese cat.

Painting and cats were her passions. Adorning several of the walls of the house with her works, many of them local, pastoral images, she would enjoy the appreciation they got as visitors fawned and complimented. Her own paintings had overshadowed those of rivals at university. As a student, she had created fairies and gorgons, most of them hidden away in the attic. Uncovered, they could inspire both awe and fear.

One painting that had terrified me as a child had shown a minotaur standing fearsome against a Grecian landscape. In shades of red acrylic, it had haunted my nightmares, and later, my dreams.

The Siamese cats, elegant and diabolical, would watch me with their periwinkle eyes. Rubbing themselves against my leg, and sitting in my lap, they would become loving fiends. Their beauty would be shattered when they laid back their heads to howl like children. Together, they would multiply, bringing in money and mess. Nevertheless, I loved those beasts.

The largest, a huge, stocky tom named Skyla, ruled the neighbour-hood with his charms. Grey-pointed and smooth furred, my father had likened him to Sean Connery. The others, sleeker and slightly narcis-sistic, would vie for my mother's affections.

My father, like my mother, was a teacher. A devotee to his subjects of history and humanities, he would travel forty miles to his work-place, the town where Sternoake was situated. A tall man, with pale skin, dark hair and green eyes, he was Celtic-looking and slightly resembled the actor Liam Neeson. He enjoyed nothing better than a walk in the fresh air, or what was left of it. His main love was the blues. With a passion, he would ignite his music with a twist of the volume, resurrecting with his touch the charms of Memphis Minnie and Robert Johnson.

In the spare room stood a grainy, black-and-white photograph of a band named Watson Browne. Years ago, he had been the singer. Although never taking the time to learn the guitar or Hammond organ, my father was a maestro on the harmonica, possessing several in his collection.

In the past, my father had been a strong yet quiet student revolu-tionary, my mother a mysterious woman of the arts. My father the working-class rocker, my mother the middle-class painter.

As children, my sisters and I had been referred to as "Russian dolls", each of us sharing similar features, yet being different in size.

Katherine, my middle sister, was a talented athlete, and head-strong. Often, when we fought, she would emerge as the winner. This got me down. Leslie, the younger, tired of being referred to as "cute" by older admirers. In aversion to this, she developed a sometimes eccen-tric dress sense and unusual taste in music, some of it inspired by Dad.

Squabbles often took place, not surprisingly.

Our whole family squabbled a lot. I was usually the loser or the dark horse due to spending so much time away from home. Often I was blamed for things I had not done, or bullied by my two sisters over my weird habits. Most of the time, I didn't even have a clue what was going on.

Among the workers at the offenders' unit, my mother had many admirers she turned down and one she didn't. This one was her boss, a short, squat man named Mark. Jokingly, she had drawn his caricature onto a Christmas card. Later, this man was to drive a wedge between our family.

Mark soon became a regular visitor to our home, driving up impressively in a vintage Morris Minor van. Sometimes he would allow my sisters and me to ride, open air, on the back. Offering me gifts, he would bring Queen albums and take me for rides in his various cars. Undoubtedly, as a friend, he won my initial affections.

Mark soon became a regular visitor to our household. Every Sunday meant fast cars and loud music. He would tell a selection of jokes. Not many of them were particularly funny, but everyone managed to sustain good humour. Like my mother, he was an animal lover, but he had a reputation for being a cruel prankster. I could only express my horror and sullen-faced lack of amusement when he drew two thick eyebrows onto Lucy's face with black marker.

As we speed fanatics rode along on the back of the van, Dad stayed indoors. Mum would squeeze into the front seat next to Mark, casually smoking through the window.

Christmas, as ever, brought conflict, only this time it was to come on a much larger scale. As the dreary bloated drunkenness of Christmas Day grew dim, the music churned itself along to the howling of the cats and the barking of the dogs. I noticed that Dad was not playing his blues. Instead, he sat slumped over the dinner table, barely touching what was left of his food. Sighing deeply over the pockmarked tablecloth, he rarely interrupted his own personal silence. Meanwhile, Mum and Mark sat laughing like happy children by the fire, the warmth of the orange coals creating flickers with each brandy-soaked smile.

"What's wrong, Dad?"

"Oh, nothing. Nothing," he said with solemn concealment. "Just Christmas. It takes it out of you."

Leslie, sulking in the corner, said nothing. Katherine had gone to bed exhausted, reluctant to change out of her new Fruit of the Loom sweater. Meanwhile, I held on loosely to the jaded tail of the celebrations, sipping slowly the bitter glass of red wine in my hand.

"Dad, Jess! Join the game of cards," urged Leslie, tiredly joining the couple beside the fire.

"I'm crap at cards. Can't be bothered," I sighed in return, taking a handful of swiftly melting chocolates from the jar.

Dad said nothing. His cigarette burnt out slowly in the ashtray.

"Dad?"

"Ooh! I got an ace!" laughed Mum, slapping Mark on the back.

"But I've still got a full hand," grinned Mark.

In the tarnished firelight, his smile made him look like a goblin. As a small child, Leslie had once run into my parents' bedroom, claiming she had seen a goblin from the window. Hugging her tightly and wiping away the fright with a warm blanket, Mum had reassured her that the hideous apparition was little more than that second-rate scaremonger, the boggart.

Mark's short, squat form, doubly compressed in girth by the shadows, seemed at that moment strangely grotesque, even ominous.

"Mark's sleeping in the spare bed tonight," announced Mum. "I hope you all said thank you to him for your presents."

Mum's caricature, from a glance, looked more like a turtle than Indiana Jones. However, it caught Mark's grimace to perfection.

Listlessly, I left to listen to Queen in my bedroom. Curiously, I decided to return less than half an hour later.

Dad had gone upstairs with a bottle of wine. Mark had retired elsewhere. Only Mum sat by the fire.

Drunkenly, she took me by the hand: "You know I believe in trust within this family," she sighed. "And I know that you all trust Mark. He's a friend. He's a good friend."

Before I could reply, she continued: "I know that you kids are all fond of Mark. Do you trust him?"

Slowly, I answered: "Yes."

"I think I am in love with Mark."

Bewildered, I went to bed. Mum stayed by the fire until it slowly extinguished itself.

As Boxing Day arrived, boldly lettered I STILL LOVE YOUs were hung in every window of the house. Worded by the pen of my father, they spelt out his loss and sincerity to no avail. My mother, although breaking out into sweat and tears, convinced herself that her decision was final. The next day, as New Year approached, Dad left the house, left the village for the town where he worked. Mark moved in. Mum put the house up for sale. Dad stayed with a friend until he could find a place of his own. My sisters became withdrawn.

When I returned to Sternoake, I hardly spoke of Christmas at all.

– TWENTY-TWO –

MY HAIR WAS AUBURN, or, to most unfortunate onlookers, ginger. Ginger hair did not suit me. I could imagine the staff using my hair as an excuse to play a more personal version of Knock Down Ginger. Through the long, dull, chocolate-brown sludge that remained of my time at home, I had spread uncomfortably over the top of my leggings. Fat and ginger.

I had asked Mum to buy me some hair dye as I had been feeling particularly dowdy that day. She had returned with the ominous-looking box, which had just added to my crash in self-esteem. Knocked down and ginger, I had returned to my room to doodle.

In all my plumpness and paranoia, I had gone on holiday to Turkey with Mum and the troll, soon to return on tickets lovingly bought by the latter.

My swimming costume was black. It had a magical little zip that concealed my expanding waistline. Nipping me under the arms, I felt a certain pleasurable masochism under its corset-like grip. My flesh, white as sour milk, seemed to seep, almost drip, from its seams. Looking in the mirror, repulsed, I stood at unusual angles, hoping to find the ideal photograph pose to conceal my insecurities before any visits to the swimming pool.

Louise was coming. Mark's slim, blonde, pampered daughter would be there to win the favour of my sisters. They idolised her, looked up to her as if she were a pop star and their best friend in one. She was cool, pretty and had a way with all the boys, including her joyriding, pill-popping partner in cool-prettiness. She seemed to shine her naturally sun-tanned light from every Reebok-clad footstep. Secretly, deep down behind the lacklustre fringe that soiled my eyes, I wished to duck her in the cold, deep waters of the swimming pool.

Lying, uncomfortably, on my bed, ignoring the book I had tried to pick up, I found myself contemplating the scene of Louise and me drowning in a tidal wave of fly-speckled chlorine. Beside the pool stood a single rescuer, male. He only had time to save one of us. Above the sea of chemically saturated beetles and twigs ticked a clock, a clock with one minute to spare. Who would be saved? Votes were cast.

Gazing out of the hotel window, I was relieved to watch the sun setting, the very colour of the Turkish delight I had sat glutting myself with for the last few hours. Beneath the balcony, disco lights were beginning to flash clumsily across the still water. Motorbikes blared their tracks across the hilltops, visible above tourist-strewn hotels. I found myself thinking of Deacon. Sam, the beautiful barman, stood smilingly content behind the bar, serving invisible customers with his Bournville-eyed swagger. Louise ran over, reluctant-yet-willing, to meet him. He had a string of concubines, she had her beloved joyrider. After a hug and a kiss, Louise ran to Mark for some more money.

Earlier that day, I had wandered past his bar clutching a large bag of shopping and several towels. Hanging my head, pondering all the self-pitying *if onlys* and *could've beens*, I had just been greeted with an instruction to "smiii-iile!".

Sam had never really liked me, unlike the aged bearded crazy who had rubbed my behind at the drinking fountain. He probably did it to anything with breasts and a vagina.

Shovelling a handful of pink sweetness into my mouth, I finally removed my costume. I pulled on some of Mum's old trousers. They were too tight. My bare arms and shoulders were an abomination. Their yoghurt-tinged surface was discoloured with purple-red blotches that resembled the surface of Mars. Earlier, I had been scolded by Katherine for picking at my scabs. I had nothing better to do. I just picked, ate and sat in my room. My book had grown soggy from lying by the pool, the Turkish delight soggier from the heat.

That evening I would have one thing to look forward to: Mum was taking me out for a meal. I was the only family member who would eat foreign food. Everyone else just lived on burgers, chips and egg sandwiches.

Earlier in the week I had experienced a small dose of adventure. Mark had taken me for a ride on a hired moped. Clinging to the bar on the back seat, I had been lashed in the face by dust as each rock swooped by beneath my shoes. As the tyres hit each groove in the road, I had been thrown into the air, landing heavily on my big backside. The feeling of weightlessness had thrilled me, the oncoming heaviness had brought me back to earth. In the air, I had seen only the clouds and the blur of the sand, not Sam and Louise.

The boat trip would also provide me with talk to bring back to Sternoake. Leslie and myself had taken to the water near the island, unafraid of the lizards and crabs, swimming through the salty tide to the shore. My saline-filled eyes had become an underwater documentary. Louise, meanwhile, preferred to sunbathe on the deck.

Simon and I would have plenty of fantastic cars to talk about on my return. Ancient Edsels, Volkswagen Beetles, Chevrolet Bel Airs and Vauxhall Vivas had driven past in their droves like a flock of beautiful, metallic animals waiting to be chased and admired. Simon had always been fond of cars, as was Deacon, only Simon was more specific to names, makes and registration plates. Together, we had sat, legs hanging over the "danger ladder" of the fort, watching over the wall as traffic came swirling around the roundabout. An entire autobahn of treasures had later greeted us from the back of the minibus as we compared X-reg bangers and rusty tail fins.

Sometimes, in the common room, I would sit drawing cars, each growing more and more elaborate, before photocopying them for Simon to add life to with his colouring pens. Deacon would imagine, then imitate, what each engine would sound like.

Sitting alone, sunburned and bloated, in my hotel room, I wished for a friendly nudge from Simon or a bear hug from Deacon. In my bag, I had some bland-tasting chewing gum. I would donate that to Neil. He might find it tasted better than I thought.

Inside a carrier bag, I had various T-shirts, most of them cheap reproductions of designer labels. Unfamiliar with the brands, I picked each one for its design and symbol, oblivious to whomever Mr Gucci was. Carefully, I had selected colours to suit Marie, Rosa and Eunice. The one I had bought for myself, white with two gold-trimmed Cs sitting back to back, had shrunk due to heat and water.

Suddenly my thoughts swerved violently away from that fragile lull of goodwill, forming a tower of justified malice. Through squinted eyes, I pictured Louise gasping for breath in the pool, her tan washing off into an oil slick that would eventually engulf her. Suffocating in orange greasiness, she could see, through chlorine-reddened eyes, the figures of both Sam and her boyfriend standing on the poolside, damning her for her infidelity.

Re-running the scene inside my head, I took the last powdery lump of Turkish delight from the bottom of the box, fingers sticky from indulgence. Cleansing my hands with shampoo, I left my room to wander onto the rooftop.

Staring down at the distantly subdued town, I saw mopeds and cars flicker across the shadows of the narrow streets. Lights and lanterns were hastily lit above the welcoming doorways of tavernas, and candles swayed beneath canvas roofs. I enjoyed my solitude.

Staying among company for long periods of time felt like confrontation. Sometimes, I felt uncomfortable due to the constant nagging, the constant criticism. The paranoia it bestowed upon me brought inside my head both a hatred of myself and a hatred of others that crossed my path. I would flee from company and revel in my own personal exile, finding a strange pleasure in my rejection. Sometimes, I craved a friendly shoulder, be it for a laugh, a cry, or just a few scraps of thrown-about conversation. People were difficult to please; yet sometimes, too accepting. Sometimes, they compelled me; yet sometimes, they repelled me. There was never a balance.

Friends could easily become enemies, and vice versa. The once-hated Eunice had now become a close friend over the sink and stereo. Marie, although closer than close, had upset me recently by roping me in for daily art and craft sessions. Normally these feelings towards individuals flickered from one extreme to another. Sometimes, I would find myself missing somebody who had been gone for only one day. At other times, I would be in company, although not entirely unpleasant, then find myself skulking away down the corridor to escape.

Company was, in some ways, like a large plate of food. After initially experiencing it, it made me uneasy before I could find it enjoyable and delicious. Then, after glutting myself with attention, I would grow increasingly nauseous, craving to cleanse myself with solitude. Some of my best moments were spent behind the door of my bedroom, shutting myself away with pen, paper and radio. Some of my worst moments were spent, after weeks alone at the tail end of the summer holidays, craving an attentive ear. Sometimes, I only craved company to recognise that I actually existed. Sometimes, I didn't want to exist at all.

Remembering Shaun's lost voice, I imagined how, at the start of a conversation, he would enthral me until the jokes became tedious. After that, I would wander into a silent crowd, tired of the subject. Sometimes, I would even tire of my own subjects. Even when indulging in much wanted talk of interests and obsessions, I could soon burn out my own tongue. My mind would sweat the obsession out, like a poison, only to later return it to my mouth for a second cleansing. Sometimes, I would indulge with others in their topics of obsession, before growing red and raw inside from the sheer repetitiveness. Like an army of Chevettes with faulty brakes, none of us could stop.

Whilst lying in bed, I would repeat and constantly alter the same story, run through like a film-show, behind my eyelids, hoping it would merge itself into a lucid dream. All of a sudden, the film-show would grind to a halt, the reels of spool growing stale. My head would empty itself like a cinema after the drama had played out. Sleep came uneasy. Tossing and turning, I would try to forget each detail before creating a new direction, usually similar to its predecessor.

If John, or Roger, Taylor failed to appear in perfect detail, I would spend my time trying to recreate their features in perfect detail before I could cast them in the starring role. If, somehow, my mind lost track of the plot, I would re-play the show from the moment I had paused. Sometimes, whole key events would be repeated several times before they were perfect.

I loved the company of the stars of my film-shows. I was the writer, director and leading actress. I could control them. I could even control the bad guys. If I became surrounded by masked assassins, I could be sure of being rescued by the hero. When a film-show became a lucid dream, things became much more interesting. The bad guys *might* harm me, there could be some *real* danger. The hero might use different lines, act against the usual flow of things. The uncertainty was chilling and thrilling, the element of surprise a boost to my imagination.

Most of these became short stories I would scribble down in my note book, or comic strips, carefully drawn and hidden under my bed.

Packing dirty clothes into my case, I checked several times if I had left anything out. Luckily, nothing was missing. The Turkish delight had now gone, leaving an empty space in the case, but a sickly feeling in my stomach. Feeling fatter than ever, I had decided that the meal tonight would be buried, but not forgotten, beneath my ever-tightening layers of size 14 clothing. I was unlikely ever to stand a chance with Sam, so it made little difference.

Mum and Mark were very much in love, or so it seemed. He bought her flowers and took her to hotels. Dad was living in a flat in the town where Sternoake stood. Mark had won me over with rides in his car, but his presence irked me still. I could not quite feel comfortable whenever he was around.

Whenever I felt uncomfortable with somebody, I would stand quite rigidly, my arms clutched tightly across my chest, my eyes focused away from the person in question: a defensive stance. Most of the time, this stance was produced subconsciously. Often, my left arm would hang down by my side, the elbow squeezed by my right hand. This allowed me the pretence of being comfortable. When nervous or uncertain, I would circle my left wrist with my right hand, squeezing the fingers tightly until they met. With Mark, I found myself repeating most of these subconscious actions, even wringing my fingers together like wet towels.

My face proved a great area of insecurity. Often, I would touch my chin, or chew my fingers lightly on their sides. I never bit my nails – they were always immaculate – but I found them near my lips at all times. Usually this happened without me knowing. It had to be pointed out. These actions must have made me look like a classic paranoiac.

Food was my biggest sense of comfort. It felt comfortable chewing something in my mouth. If I fell into boredom or listlessness, I would return, satisfied, to my room with confectionery. Denying myself this comfort had taken a great deal of willpower, this willpower and denial in return providing a different form of satisfaction: the comfortable feeling of being in control. Now I knew I was out of control, thinking of food at every point of the day.

Many of Sternoake's residents found food to be a comfort factor. Elena's tasks were set around food, this being her reward. Simon and Peter were promised second helpings if they had been on their best behaviour. All the residents seemed to look forward to breakfast, lunch and dinner. Supper was almost a party with its novelty array of snacks. Many, such as Sabrina, returned from their holidays overweight due to their parents' incentive of offering food as rewards. Often, food was stolen from cupboards and gorged upon in secret. Food was a universal pleasure as opposed to a means of staying alive.

At various birthday parties, hungry or not, plates would be filled until towers of sacred nuggets seemed to topple before they hit people's laps. Often, although nauseous from over-indulgence, the consumer would continue eating to the point of damage. As the monthly weigh-ins were recorded eagerly by the staff with their electric scales, an increase of over twelve pounds was not unusual.

Food tasted good, tasted nice: that was how the young people perceived it. Oblivious to the threats of obesity or losing their looks, they enjoyed its feel on their tongues, its taste, its smell, the large gatherings of it that concealed the surface of their plates. Food was a friend that never said "no".

I found it hard to refuse. My willpower had gone. It would take me far too long to lose the two stone I had gained in the last year. A vicious circle had surrounded me: I was fat, I felt unhappy with this, then ate more for solace. I did not need to eat as much as I did, and usually I enjoyed each large mouthful far too much. I did not *need* to be so heavy. My weight had grown as punishment for such indulgences.

My indulgences had continued in Turkey. With no chance of any holiday romance, no admirers waiting by my door, all my friends left back at home, my loneliness craved fulfilment. Food was both a close friend and a hated enemy. Guilt always followed the short-lived pleasure of its sticky taste. Pleasure turned into fat. The fatter I got, the more I craved. My Turkish delight was gone.

– TWENTY-THREE –

"CONGRATULATIONS!" RANG THE voices throughout the garden. "Jessica is soon to be a college girl!"

Sulking, I received a hastily designed, yet sincerely crafted, certificate. Admiring the valiant efforts taken by Vince and Simon, nevertheless I hung my head in dread at the anticipation of enrolment. Soon my world would be split into two separate kingdoms: the kingdom of Sternoake and the kingdom of college. I would have to conceal my dual nationality. If people at college knew I went to a "special school", I would be outed as a freak.

"Just think of all the nice lads you'll meet," enthused Stacey, rolling her tongue with comic precision.

"Just think of all the bogs I'll be hiding in," I murmured, unheard.

"Soon to be a college girl! Soon to be a college girl!"

The whole mock-celebration seemed to stink of American sit-coms. I didn't bother to even fake a smile.

"If you wanted rid of me," I piped out, "why didn't you just shoot me instead of sending me out into exile? Why don't you have me dead instead of just…half gone? Half gone for mucking up your nice, clean unit!"

Shaun, had he been around, would have savoured my words.

College was a *normal* place, full of *normal* people. The probability was that I would not fit in. As soon as I was to enter the hall of enrolment, I would keep my head down and my mouth shut, then there would be no reason for them to mock me. I would wear a mask of normality, concealing my true, Asperger's-tainted nature from all. At Sternoake, nothing I did could be classed as too weird, there were many with behaviour much stranger than my own; but college was the real world, the normal world.

Academically, I knew I could pass the exams without much problem, but socially I would struggle. I found it hard to work in a group, to listen, concentrate and communicate at the same time. However, I promised myself that I would make an effort.

Suddenly I felt singled out, isolated: "How come none of the other young people have to be sent to college?"

"Because you are our most able student," replied Vince with a flourish. "Besides, you are sixteen, and most sixteen-year-olds are studying for their GCSEs."

"Why can't I just study them here?"

"Because we don't have the facilities," replied Stacey, cutting in.

In reality, they wanted me to have the social experience along with the academic.

"I'll be there to accompany you to classes," offered Roisin, knowing I would need a partner to help fend off my insecurities. "On other days, when I'm teaching Group Four, you'll have Zia."

"Yeah! I can pose as a mature styooooodent!" grinned Zia, flashing her teeth from under her Ray Bans sunglasses.

Zia was one of those alarmingly confident people who seemed to strut through life like a cat. Beneath her bouncing halo of black curls, the sheen of those infamous Ray Bans seemed to reflect the very glow of her confidence as she smiled her wide smile. Surprisingly, Zia had once been shy. Confidence had built itself around her, like a protective wall, during her days studying drama, before soaking into the person beneath, lodging itself within every pore. Now, swaggering and assured, her confidence was now for real, no longer just a show.

Zia was naturally loud and outspoken, my perfect seating partner for English studies. Also a bit of a mathematical genius, she would aid me in the perils of equations. Roisin, more artistically inclined, would travel the distance with me to the art block.

Mr Burbridge, the art lecturer, reminded me of a retired rugby player gone to seed. I imagined that, following his demise from the game, he had replaced his banded shirt with a comfy sweater. It was *always* the same sweater. Brown, tinged with green, like mildewed beef stew, and striped with ribbons of faded heather, it wrapped itself tightly around his shoulders and stomach seemingly refusing to let go. From its branches of unwound wool hung assorted flora of Sellotape ends and tiny glimmers of dried up Marvin glue. His mouth, forever examining works with gruff and grunting commentary, seemed gummed up at the edges by what looked like a mixture of cream and spittle. I imagined he had been eating a Cadbury's Creme Egg, then forgotten to wipe his face.

Burbridge was an ardent fan of still-life drawing and painting. Often he would line up displays of difficult, intertwining lines of foliage or hard, angular structures composed of bricks, pipes and corrogated iron. Then there were the various animal bones and plastic fruits. He piled these up hoping for each unfortunate artist to capture the unseen shadows of each item. His favourite piece was the lobster pots. A huge mesh of interlaced wicker and seaweed, this proved the most difficult to recreate with pencil, paper and brush.

On my own attempt at the lobster pots, I found myself frustrated at my unsuccessful efforts, gradually losing all interest in the matter. The resulting piece scored a low-flying "D".

Laurence Peters, the master of mathematics, was different to Burbridge in presence, voice and stature. Tall, gangly and red-haired, he was a natural target for underground mockery and shared wit from his students. Immaculately presented in crisply ironed white shirts and slacks that hung uncomfortably loose from his prominent hip-bones, he would scrawl unfathomable notes across the whiteboard with his marker pen. His voice, high, shrill and unwittingly camp, sometimes deepened when he addressed certain logic problems with verve. He seemed young for his age and position, and seemed to be a confused adolescent in his early thirties.

The English leaders, for both language and literature, were two likeable middle-aged women named Pat and Jill. Pat, dark-haired and dressed like a lady of the countryside, would read the class *Animal Farm* with great vigour, often joining in with each student over their individual grief concerning the death of Boxer, the brave carthorse, who we later found out to be a symbol of the repressed Russian proletariat. Jill, grey-haired and fair, introduced us to the delights of Oscar Wilde. Often chatting to the students in small groups before the class began, she would share her views on anything from literature to the benefits of buying a bicycle.

Together we studied J.B. Priestley's *An Inspector Calls*. Initially, it proved a much-talked-about whodunnit, but beneath the surface of such thrills lay a more solemn, political, message. Eva Smith, a young working-class girl, the suicide in question, provided the catalyst of the play. The contented, middle-class Birling family, smug and comfortable in their position, interrupted suddenly by the mysterious, and seemingly spectral, Inspector Goole, were all in some way to blame for her death.

I found myself playing the unsympathetic and cold-hearted charity worker, Sybil Birling, the mother of the family. Naturally, I added tones of British soap opera to her voice in class dramatisation. I took on the role with great venom. A girl named Amelia, who had befriended me, took on the part of Sybil's guilt-ridden daughter, Sheila.

Later in the course, we watched the black-and-white movie, starring Alec Guinness as the naive and irresponsible Eric Birling.

Amelia was close to another girl named Kerry. The two of them would meet up with Zia and me at breaks in the canteen. Sometimes, from the corners of our eyes, we would spy a boy named Gerald.

Gerald, who studied maths with us, was small, slight of build and blond. He reminded me of Take That star Mark Owen. On first impressions, he was friendly and eager to know me. That was when I first became infatuated.

Some days we would walk home together, with Roisin or Zia casting a wary eye. On other days, I would signal to him as I rode past in Zia's car. At night I would dream about him. During lectures I had the promise of seeing him, there behind his desk, borrowing my ruler at will.

Gerald's friend, James, had a bumfluff moustache. He shared his calculator with me, even when I didn't need it. Roisin and Zia both thought he fancied me. I was a disbeliever. He was attractive, in a very "blokey" kind of way, but I was far too infatuated with Gerald. When James asked me out, I accepted. It was the first offer I had ever had.

His Halloween party went with a proper riot. James played his heavy metal records loud until the neighbours complained. Later, in fancy dress as a witch, I went upstairs with him to watch *Bram Stoker's Dracula*. He liked Winona Ryder, but she was much slimmer and prettier than me. He said he liked girls with brown eyes and I was flattered. Around my neck I wore a gothic crucifix. Although ardently an atheist, I told him it was to keep away vampires. Secretly, I longed to be bitten by a vampire, to become one myself, to have eternal youth and mystique. James was dressed as one. That night, I found him incredibly attractive. I had also swallowed down an entire bottle of Scrumpy Jack.

James had a lot in common with me. He liked similar music and similar T.V. shows. I never told him I had Asperger's syndrome: I thought it would put him off me. Nobody at college knew I had it: I thought it would put them off me too. I was "normal", if a little reclusive. With my head held low, I had a secretive air. I must have looked troubled or paranoid in some way. James believed, in his usual heroic way, that he could look after me. I almost felt safe.

James lived only a few strides away from Dad's flat. It was so easy to reach him. James got on well with Dad, although he had never liked football.

Dad was a devoted follower of Manchester City. Most Manchester United fans, he thought, were there only for the glory or taken by the merchandising that seemed to be springing up everywhere. Dad followed every game on the radio, or on *Match of the Day*.

He would also enjoy listening to the news, current affairs, or political broadcasts. Most of these were on during breakfast time when conversation was impossible. I did not have my own bedroom: the flat was too small, but Dad let me sleep in his bed above the sitting room whilst he slept on the couch. There were African masks on the walls, belongings left by the last occupant. Dad liked them: he had always taken an interest in other cultures. He did not mind the small flat, with its mildew-patterned bathroom, the only real *room* that existed. He took simple pleasures and was never one for needing luxury.

This frustrated me. However, Dad let me have the freedom and independence whilst under his roof that Sternoake had never granted me.

Dad, James and I made quite a family. We could have been happy, but I was constantly thinking of Gerald.

Obsessively, I would follow him around the halls of the college, offering to buy him a drink from the canteen, asking if he needed to borrow any of my equipment. Gerald, naturally shy and sparse with his conversation, would usually only answer in monosyllables.

In winter, this changed. After remaining "friends" with James, I was now free to pursue Gerald as often as I pleased. Together after a maths lesson, we walked down to the crossroads together. Wandering down the steep bank, through a shallow snowdrift, feeling it melt and crunch beneath my feet, I ignored the cold, seeking only to be beside my target.

After an uneasy conversation, I found that he and his sister shared a love of teeny-pop bands. This was a slight knock back to his picture of perfection: a man who liked teeny-pop bands was not exactly macho. Later, he explained that he only liked the music because his sister did. She dressed in grunge attire, wore a Nirvana T-shirt, hiding her true interests in Robbie Williams, Jason Orange and the gang. Gerald then told me that he had dyed his blond hair black because all his friends loved Morrissey.

After telling him of my fondness for The Lemonheads and Bjork, I found that my mouth may have been sprouting my adoration of Mark Owen. This, however, might have frightened him due to his obvious resemblance to the star. Besides, some days I tried not to like Take That as most people thought they were naff. Anyway, I sometimes found Robbie Williams annoyed me.

We were both virgins. Naturally, I acknowledged my own virginity all too much. Sex at Sternoake would have been the highest of crimes, higher than glue-sniffing or even rat-poisoning. My copies of *More* magazine were regularly confiscated due to their safe-sex articles and naughty *Position of the Fortnight* guides. If a film was rented, it was to have no nudity or hints at copulation, hence we usually watched *The Sound of Music* or *Free Willy* on Uncle Derek's recommendation. Ironically, I found much amusement in the title of the latter.

Neither of us would have had sex anyway. I was too fat and insecure, he too slight, beautiful and insecure.

Still overweight, I applied my make-up badly. Zia often commented on my poor use of plum eye-shadow and mauve lipstick. Most days I went bare-faced, constantly aware of the sickly oiliness of my complexion. Mike had told me I had skin like the lard on a corned beef hash. I had wanted to punch him, but had held myself back for fear of the penalty that would be later put upon me. My hair had reverted to its usual greasy bob, an alice band sometimes holding back the straggly fringe from my poorly-plucked eyebrows. I had been flattered that James had been attracted. That was probably why I had formed a short-lived relationship with him: through sheer vanity.

I rarely went into pubs. Sternoake feared for my "safety" within the community. I looked forward to the holidays. Then I could go home to Dad's flat. There I could drink, with his more easy-going permission. I was no longer as overprotected as I was at Sternoake.

When I did dress up, it was always in loose-fitting shirts and occasionally a modest, calf-length skirt. Amelia and Kerry drew most of the attention whilst I sat, anonymously, waiting for eyes to fall my way.

Losing empathy with many of those at Sternoake, the bangers, the twiddlers, the non-verbals, I read my magazines. Many of these contained pictures of women I could never emulate. Supermodels were at their peak of world domination, body-fascism excluding all the regular freaks such as the short, the plump, the pimpled, the buck-toothed, those scarred with the natural stretch-marks of impending womanhood, and those pitiful creatures, the truly obese, whose waistlines overspilled a size ten. In despair, I was captivated by the preaching of those gurus of diet and beauty, standing by the mirror each night at odd angles trying to convince myself that I was "generously curvaceous" as opposed to the fashion dictation of the superwaif. Beneath the tangled rope of jewellery that hung around my neck and the deep red dye that bled little life into my hair, I would tear myself apart inside.

One night, I was granted permission from Eva to stay up until eleven. A documentary about the modelling business was being shown on ITV.

Seated and sweating at the thought of my own deformities, I lapsed into a low sigh of depression. Eva, hearing this moan of self-hatred, swiftly directed me to my bedroom. Refusing to leave my seat, I was ordered.

Sitting on my bed, I noticed that my room-mate lay asleep. Scuttling over towards the wardrobe, I knew that Joan Hart always slept as if comatose. No amount of noise or action could ever wake her: she even had trouble waking at fire drills. Reaching out for my wooden-heeled sandals, the soles heavy and hard-edged, I sat bolt upright with one in my hand. Bringing it down like a cleaver, I failed in slicing my leg, only bruising it.

They were no longer *my* legs, just two fat, white, sluggish appendages. They were worthy of such punishment.

On the second attempt I sliced open the pasty skin, superficially grazing through the layer of fat that had accumulated there. Repeatedly, I battered the left before moving on to the right. With each blow, my satisfaction grew. Imperfect, I would punish each imperfection, these sallow chunks of freakish meat that had caused me such unhappiness.

Slowly, Joan awoke, opening the door to walk to the bathroom. Eva, watching over the girls' corridor, heard the noise of my actions through the door-crack. Sent downstairs to stand with my back to the wall, my magazines were confiscated until I could behave like a "sensible" young woman.

Outraged, I began to cry. Tears of vanity became suspect. I was a play actress.

"I was carrying out justice!" I screamed, swallowing salt. "My legs...*those* legs...had offended me!"

"Whose legs?"

"Those legs!" I said, pointing at my own.

"Whose legs?"

"Mine," I sobbed reluctantly. "My legs. But I never asked to be born with them."

"Listen here!" shouted Eva, losing all patience. "Just thank your lucky stars that you've actually *got* legs!"

"I don't want them!"

"You're lucky you've got legs!" she yelled again. "Some people don't have legs! They've lost them through injury, or they're born without them. Just be glad you're not in a wheelchair like those people. Be glad you're not *physically* disabled."

"I wish I *was* in a wheelchair. Then people wouldn't notice that I'm fat."

— TWENTY-FOUR —

STERNOAKE WAS A place of order, a place of routine, a place of enforced safety. To eat toast without butter or to use salts instead of foam in the bath were actions considered "wrong". Young people were trained, on arrival, towards the existence of a normal life, at least superficially so. "Please" and "thank you", the ever-popular beginnings and ends of sentences, were encouraged with prompts to the point where a request or comment was considered obsolete without their inclusion. All residents would greet company in the common room each morning with "good morning", repeated meaninglessly on autopilot. It was an enforced method of acting "normal". Acting was what it was.

"Normal" people apparently liked vacuuming, absolutely adored washing up dirty dishes, and were always courteous towards visitors and superiors. Superiors were there to protect us, to shelter us from the perils of the outside world, yet they wrote us programmes for road safety and handed us fill-in sheets on how to buy a tin of beans.

Superior-superior people sat in the office all day, the office from which all young people were barred, although Simon often sneaked inside to fill his pockets with leftover custard creams. Thursday was a visitors' meeting. All the dirty cups and plates were handed to those on kitchen duties, including myself.

Upstairs in my room, homework needed to be done. As I was confined to the kitchen, I would have to finish the essays, unfortunately, during break. As the manageress of Sternoake smiled past, handing me another tray of work to be done, something inside me snapped. As she fawned back towards the office, I clutched the tray with pent-up rage. I had already served her enough. Smashing the tray and its feeble contents down, hard, against my leg, I play-stumbled convincingly enough to persuade people it was an "accident".

"Oh dear!"

"Right!" drilled Eva. "Clean up all that broken mess! Then we'll see how much china you'll have to pay for."

"I have no money!"

"Rubbish! What about your disability allowance?"

"I'm saving up for a holiday! Yes, a holiday out of here! Away from this bloody place!"

"At the way you're going, you wouldn't be trusted on a plane abroad."

"But you trust me enough to go to college."

Reluctantly, yet with no shame or remorse, I scooped the china into the bin.

"Can I have a plaster for my leg?" I enquired.

"The china needs clearing up first!"

"What's more important?" I asked, cornering her with my glare. "Some old rich person's china, or a young girl's bad knee?"

"That's not relevant."

The real world was a world where young people of my age drank in pubs, legal or not, and went around to each other's houses after college to play music and swap gossip. Amelia and Kerry never had to clean the manageress's dishes, unless of course they were paid to do so at a restaurant. They didn't have staff. They had parents.

After a weekend at my parents' house, between circumstances avoiding Mark, I had dyed my hair a deep mahogany with the aid of Leslie, who was, at present, a blonde. Uncle Derek had not approved. Mum, however, said I looked like Cher. For the first time in months, I felt more attractive. As the dye had faded, so had my confidence. However, Sternoake disapproved of me dying my hair in any of *their* bathrooms, even if I did promise to clear up all my mess and put the bottles in the bin.

If I was caught inside Sternoake wearing make-up, I faced trouble. If I wanted to go out alone, as opposed to on a group outing, I was dis-allowed. A few times I planned to abscond from college so I could walk into town with Amelia and Kerry. Roisin had once allowed me to do this, claiming it was "good practice for learning social skills".

The two faces I wore were very different. At Sternoake, I was outspoken, slightly rebellious, prone to moods and usually true to myself. At college, I kept my true nature hidden beneath the mask of the shy girl who never gossiped or giggled, never showed up late and was never rude to colleagues.

On the surface, to the outside world, I was a nice girl, a good girl, a pushover. Others outside would never guess that I broke china, or swore frequently, or cried out when germs touched my skin. I was small, mousy and softly-spoken. I was like a little girl who wanted to get on with the big girls at school.

During class hours, I found myself coated by this shell. As it covered me, like a nun's habit, I found my inner emotions being pushed to the bottom of my stomach. Returning home, dead on time at five o'clock, I found they would erupt from me like a firework inside a volcano. I would get in trouble, but not show myself up. Marie and Eva said I was turning into a "Jekyll and Hyde".

Sitting on my bed with my homework during break, I pictured the cartoon images of a tiny devil on one of my shoulders, a tiny angel on the other. At college, I was super-normal. At Sternoake I was mad. Naturally, I was worried should Amelia, Kerry or, worse still, Gerald see this "Hyde side". If that happened, then college would become like school. At school, I had been the local freak show, the subject of "witch hunts" and jokes. At school, I had sometimes wondered if I would've been better off dead. Nobody would find out about my past, I decided. Nobody would *ever* find out that I lived at Sternoake. I knew that I could be a good actress and I would continue to live this life-lie I had created.

I told Amelia and Kerry that I could not go out because my mother was a strict Catholic and was very overprotective. At other times, I would say that I was babysitting my little cousin. Gradually, the lies tangled themselves into a sticky cobweb of complications. Amelia had seen me walking through the doors of Sternoake. Before she had even taken notice or asked questions, my lies leapt to the defence. I told her

I worked there. When Kerry asked why Roisin and myself always arrived on time, together, I told her we had both agreed, in the staff room, to do the course together: Roisin as a mature student, myself because I needed the qualifications.

I felt like an outsider on both sides of the wall. Because of college, I had been excluded from the Sternoake Christmas play. Instead, I was forced to devote more time to my studies. At college, I was excluded from the social circle outside timetables because I had to return home at five for "evening activities". These, too, were timetabled, the schedule compulsory. Sternoake was a monument to schedule. If your name was on the list for a certain activity at a certain time, then you had to do it: willing or not.

One Thursday evening, missing out on the chance to drink with Amelia and Kerry, I found my name, along with that of every female staff and young person, penned down for *knit and natter*. Instead of following the will of Uncle Derek, who had penned himself down for *fish and chips on the seafront* along with most of the male residents, I questioned his management skills.

"Derek?" I trilled with mock-naivety. "What does *knit and natter* mean?"

"It means," he explained, puffing out his freshly-ironed chest, "that all you lasses will be sitting in the common room knitting and nattering. If you're lucky, you can watch *EastEnders*."

Joy. I hated *EastEnders*.

"Why are there no lasses going to the seafront? And why are none of the lads knitting or nattering?"

"Because," he said, towering over me, making me feel grotesquely short, "I thought it would be nice if all the lads had a break together, and all the lasses sat in and relaxed."

"But knitting un-relaxes me."

"The others seem to like it."

The "others" did not like knitting. They only knit through its familiarity. Since kindergarten the needles and wool had been forced into their hands.

"Anyway…" I paused for effect, "I can't knit."

"Nonsense!" laughed Uncle Derek with a boom. "Every lass knows how to knit!"

"Well here's one that doesn't. And if she tries, then she drops the needles," I said in return. "Oh, what a shame that I am so, so, so crap at knitting. I suppose it's going to knock me back in any career I wish to take. Oh bugger! Now I can't be a journalist or car salesperson! And all because I can't knit!"

"Now, now. I think we'll have a little less of that attitude!"

Twirling my knitting needles around like batons before mock-stabbing myself in the chest, I entertained the bored, and not particularly nattering, knitters.

Eva, in charge of the select few, sat, needles on lap, unmoved and gazing at repeats of *EastEnders*.

"I'm bored," sighed Rhiona.

"Derek's out of the building," I smiled knowingly.

Joan Hart's face immediately lit up. Joan, a large, clumsy girl, was my room-mate. Normally quiet, a smile meant that her internal supply of mischief was beginning to surface. Her mother still cut her hair. Joan knew little of the art of protesting. However, today she was defiant, letting her needles and yarn drop to the floor. She arose from her seat to turn on the radio.

"See? We're all bored," I told Eva, between the twin bald domes of the Mitchell brothers. "I suggest we make alternative plans for while Del-boy's away."

"Play *Chase Joan Around Building*!" hollered Joan, springing gawkily into the air.

"Yeah!" screamed Rhiona. "Let's chase Joan!"

Soon, we all began chasing Joan around the building. Each time she was caught, she let out a loud scream. In the dark, I likened the action to a scene from one of Anita's favourite Hammer films. Marie was crowned champion, pinning down Joan the record number of times. Joan herself played the victim with aplomb.

As Derek returned, to his dismay, no knitting had been done.

"The girls got sidetracked," explained Eva, standing above a laughing Joan Hart. "Something more important came up."

— TWENTY-FIVE —

THE HOLIDAYS LOOMED ahead. To me, even the word *holiday* suggested anything but. I would have to work extra hard to survive the regime of Mark. He had taken over the household, forcing Leslie into unwilling submission, Katherine into grouching conflict and Mum into a lull of false, alcohol-induced security. Presents and car rides had been replaced by orders and the threat of cruel practical jokes. Mark's practical jokes were neither practical nor jokes. They were never particularly funny, especially for the victim, and raised more paranoia than laughs. I never laughed at Mark's jokes. In return, he labelled me a "misery". I was used to it by now.

Packing my bags, I knew that in two days time I would be home from Sternoake. Simon was also packing his bags.

"Simon!" called Eva. "Don't forget to pack your wellies!"

"Right!" he called, cheerfully checking his case.

Sorting through his clothes, Eva searched his pockets with customs-level awareness.

"Simon Hirst, what's this?" she enquired, pulling out several toy cars, a Gameboy cover, a tube of Smarties and an Arsenal keyring.

"Things," he sighed.

"Are they *your* things?" she probed, adding a plastic digital watch to the list.

"Yeah, 'cos they're in me pocket."

"But I don't think they *belong* in your pocket!" snapped Eva.

"Ow! Gettoff! Or I'll call back that bonny old Shaun Rogers! 'E'll sort you out!"

"Simon. Enough! Did you steal them?"

"No," he sighed. "I borrowed them."

Later, I found out, through various rumours, that Simon had stolen them to take home with him. As he had no allowance with which to buy his brother, Dan, a birthday present, he had reverted to stealing. It seemed logical: steal from the staff, give to the poor. Robin Hood Junior was at work again.

Eva, on admiring his virtuous motives, let him off with just half a sheet of lines.

"Jessica!" called Marie from down the corridor. "Elena's going to Temperance Hall this afternoon. We're trying to bring more young people in the bus so it'll look more like a holiday to her."

Could a holiday be spent in a hospital?

"I'll come," I replied with curiosity. I had always wondered what sort of place Temperance Hall was.

As the bus drove away, containing Elena, Eva, Marie, Richie, Peter, Sebastian and myself, I watched the scenery roll past. Like a reel of film, I saw through the glass as towns turned into cities, cities turned to countryside, and countryside turned into smoking factory chimneys. Passing through a large industrial area, I imagined Temperance Hall to be nearby. It would be a solid, grey cube of regular, honed concrete, housing sterilised air and cold, whitewashed walls. The nurses would be faceless beings, clad also in grey, Elena the only splash of colour, blossoming pink like a tiny chrysanthemum against her pallid surroundings.

As the bus continued its journey, I found I was wrong. Once the industrial mesh of town and valley crumbled away into a tiny hillside path, I saw a large, wood-panelled building, designed like an oversized cottage, reveal itself. Courted by smaller buildings and outhouses, it lay among trees and gardens in the shade of a large wood overlooking the vicinity. The site, however, was unusually silent.

Inside there were no lost, confused patients, only a hallway leading to a children's playroom and nursery. Would they put Elena in with the children? Elena, silent, clung to Eva's arm. She knew nobody there, and if she did, there were no familiar faces for her to warm to. Elena would be alone throughout her stay. That was what frightened her.

As Elena skulked down the corridor, she cried as we said our goodbyes.

Climbing back into our seats, we waved at her through the window. Half-heartedly, she only stared back.

As I returned to my home other than Sternoake, I found the holidays passed slowly. As I revised between Mark's unfunny hilarity and shouting, I found myself missing Gerald again.

There was a huge difference between a poster and a person, as I had learned with Kieran. A poster of a pop star, actor or footballer, hung in celebrity status upon the wall, could not talk or listen. You could only imagine it did. It was true that I could talk to the paper icon, high on its shrine, sharing all my secrets, woes and desires, wishing for the picture to come to life. It was not real, no matter how hard I wished. Rhiona used to watch an old A-ha video where a comic book character came to life in true fantasy fashion. That was the stuff of daydreams, yet I still continued my worship.

Gerald could hear, see and be offended or pleased. With him, I was forced to live within my shell.

As the snow fell, Mark kept the central heating off. It was colder inside the old farmhouse than outside in the frozen fields. The house had not been decorated yet and still had an antique air about it. There were even rumours that it was haunted. Mark had added gore and monsters to the story in order to frighten Leslie.

Lucy lay across my feet, keeping them warm. Louise was staying, along with her boyfriend. I kept out of their way. As darkness fell, I mummified myself inside the sheets, wishing I could feel warm inside.

– TWENTY-SIX –

JEALOUSY HAD ALWAYS been the devil on my shoulder. This devil could be triggered by the most peculiar attributes of those who surrounded me. Along with the more obvious envies of good looks, talent and popularity, I also envied timidity and helplessness. In truth, I could be jealous of anyone, and for any amount of time.

On her arrival at Sternoake, Rosie would, on first appearances, seem immune to this devil: she was far from tall (standing only four foot ten in flat shoes) was prone to slouching and had difficulty stringing a single intelligible sentence together. Her clothes were bought by her mother, her hair cut also by her mother, and, in moments of anxiety, she would bite her hands until they bled. As a result, they were scarred and callused. Her entire life would be spent in an institution. It was the devil of her helplessness that dragged me into the trap.

As she was welcomed, with overripe warmth and enthusiasm, into the disinfected corridors of Sternoake, I found myself standing aside from the flock, like an uninvited wedding guest. My own welcoming had been a slightly less joyous occasion. Female staff queued up in their droves just to plait her hair or adorn her with make-up. Rosie was naturally, naturally pretty, and so, so impishly petite! I was five foot five inches tall and solid-yet-healthy with combination skin and greasy hair. Rosie had this sweet little way of chattering thrown-about words which simply tinkled off her tongue. I had a "foul mouth", rancid from forbidden language.

Flavour of the week, month, and possibly even the next year coming, Rosie was unstoppable in her conquest of the staff's attentions. Staff would sit and chatter her praises as they tidied her bedroom. Meanwhile, I would be clattering up the stairs with a vacuum cleaner on instructions to remove the mess from my bedroom. Whilst she was taken on shopping trips and bus rides, I would be sat behind a desk at college, studying biology. Sometimes, if she dared stray into my room, my *territory*, by mistake, I would swear at her, hoping she understood the insult. I wanted to break her Tinkerbell world of sweetness and light, to trample on those ballerina toes until they were unfit for dancing with. I wanted to break the wings of her living fairytale.

I was jealous of her innocence. She was seventeen, like myself, but had the innocent viewpoint of an infant. Kath, the classroom assistant, likened her to an angel at times. I was full of devils. She was never *bad*, only *naughty*.

Rosie was innocent to the threats of society, innocent of the bad in people, their perceptions and their faults. I felt decades older than she was, a veteran of all the evils in humanity. Whilst she was the shining piece of stardust, I was a tarnished penny. When walking to the shops, accompanied by staff as usual, she would stop and talk to strangers. In return, the stranger would usually smile, turn around and indulge in Rosie's broken sticks of conversation. She feared nobody and trusted all. Had I talked to strangers, they would have thought I was on drugs or carted me off to the nearest nuthouse.

Strangers never thought badly of her so she never knew that they could be bad people. She never knew wrong, or possibly even perceived that evil thoughts could exist. When she bit her hands, she was aware of the pain, but never suffered from the thought of the cruel world that existed around her. Sometimes, in moments of deep resentment and bitterness, I would wonder how she would react to an unwelcome reply from one of her adoring strangers. A candy-coated shell of innocence protected her. She said no wrong, and felt no wrong in return.

"She's as pure as a little snow angel," Kath would sigh, wishing that some of Sternoake's more volatile or boisterous residents were similar.

"And I'm the snow that got pissed on," I sighed beneath my breath.

"Jessica! Mind your language!"

Rosie was familiar with bad language. She had heard it from older relatives.

"Bloodeee freeeezen! Et's bloodeee freeeezen!" she would twirl with sugar-coated vowels. "Eeeeeeh! Whatyer doin? Bloodeee freeeezen! It's bloodeee cold!"

Rhiona took it upon herself to educate Rosie in the usage of the F-word and the C-word. Once, she managed to say "bollocks", but its slippage from the syrup of her tongue raised only an affectionate applause of laughter.

"Damn you! Damn you! Oooh! Let's bollocks you."

A hug and a rapture of giggles.

"I fuckin' taught her that!" beamed Rhiona with pride, failing to notice the shadowy form of Kath behind the landing door.

"Rhiona! Jessica!" she snapped. "I've had enough of you two using foul language to corrupt our Rosie!"

"But I can't help it!" pleaded a manic Rhiona. "I have Tourette's!"

"A bloodeee damn mess to ya! A bloooodeeee damn mess!"

Rosie did not know what she was saying. To her, she could be meaning "sunny" instead of "bloody". Even her speech, each word that made up her conversation, seemed to have no meaning. She knew names, such as "Kath", "Rhiona" and "Marie", and objects such as cars, houses and puppies, and terms like "lovely" and "messy", but most meanings escaped her. Sentences would be stored in her memory, then played back in the wrong order at the wrong speed. However, Rosie was certainly able in one aspect of conversation: she loved to talk.

She spoke in her own bizarre language, rarely understood but always listened to. Words were like ornaments to her feelings. If she became upset, nobody would know why. She did not know how to express her anxieties, save for her hand-chewing. As a result, her lips always brought joy but her hands always wore gloves.

My jealousy had its motives. Rosie could say anything and receive fondness in return. I had to search inside my head very carefully for words appropriate to the conversation. Occasionally, I could reel out a long string of black humour, but only among those who shared my humour. Rosie could say anything to raise a smile. Rosie could be natural at all times. I needed to be artificial. My survival instinct at college made me choose words only to please others, to protect me from isolation. Rosie could be Rosie at all times.

If I chose to act like Rosie, that would only make my behaviour yet more artificial. I would be playing the role of an innocent, yet I had no innocence inside. I had been called "sweet" and "lovely" at college, but only due to my acting skills. My life-lie was, in truth, a masterpiece. I actually found the comments patronising, but I did not wish to reveal my true, more volatile, nature.

When I could feel the real me trying to break free, I would run to the toilets with a "migraine". Lately, I had been suffering from a lot of "migraines". One student had actually suggested I go and see a doctor. Inside the toilet cubicle, I would make sure the door was securely locked before beating it violently with my fists. On my return, I would place my hands in my pockets, force a smile and try to look as unruffled as possible.

In that respect, Rosie and I shared something. We both hurt ourselves physically when we could not reveal the hurt inside. However, due to the jealousy that ruled me in her presence, I remained bitter and unfriendly towards her.

"You are turning into a bitch and a bully!"

"I'm never a bitch at college, Stacey."

"Then why can't you act here like you do at college?"

If I had, then my brain would have imploded. Sometimes, I pondered the fact that I might have been insane.

"You need to control your mood swings!" my mother would warn me.

Day after day, I would try. If a day passed with no outbursts, no Hydes, I would congratulate myself inside. On some days there were more "migraines" than on others. Nobody at college knew Hyde, only Jekyll.

Most bitches were hurting inside, they would pull others down to their level by trampling on them with comments. I could not fight myself, so like the classic bitch, I would fight and bully others. My bitchcraft was uncontrollable. Often, I did not hate the person I insulted, I was only angry with myself. Sometimes even close friends suffered the force of my temper. This was not deliberate, it just happened. Bitches aren't born, they just *become*.

Vince called my outbursts "flashpoint behaviour". He told me that this was the reason so many footballers were red-carded. On the pitch, in response to a trivial comment or gesture, they would blow up with emotion, as a result being penalised. I identified with this. If invisible God had been a referee, then my life would be scattered with red cards.

If something was changed without me knowing, I would go off like a screaming bomb. Some staff would even say: "Red card!" Soon, I grew to see the humour. If I began to seethe with rage, I would shout: "Send me off! I'm having a hypermania!"

"Off to an early bath!" Vince would reply. "And a three-match ban!"

Hanging my head in comedy style, I would lumber to my room whilst waiting for my mood to lift.

I never took anything trivially, unless it didn't interest me. Affected by the slightest little crack in the flow of my life, I would either weep uncontrollably, swear and curse with anger or, if it involved one of my favourite obsessions, laugh and hug people uncontrollably. On days when I was overcome by this obsessive joy, I would take this hugging to the extreme. Vince joked that I was a "nymphomaniac"! The people I hugged the most were usually the people I trusted the most.

Despite this, I never hugged people at college. It was my real self who did the hugging, not the life-lie. The life-lie was mainly emotionless. I usually acted like one of the Stepford Wives: perfectly nice and eager to please, but slightly robotic and humourless.

My real self sometimes raised her head, quite embarrassingly, during the everlasting boredom of three-hour art sessions. I was no good at still lives, and the tedium spawned a desperation within me. On one occasion, I clumsily spilt red paint all over my hands. On first impulse I wanted to cry with embarrassment, but instead of giving myself a "migraine", I made a joke, a typical "Jessica joke". Standing there in a crucifix position, the paint running down my wrists, I bawled the theme tune to *Jesus Christ Superstar.*

Another time, as everybody sat, bored, around the table, scribbling down sketches of lobster pots, I raised a debate about the elderly. As I discussed my reasons for being in favour of euthanasia, I reeled out a black monologue: "As an apple grows old, it begins to rot from the inside out. As the core starts to turn brown, the skin around it wrinkles and decays. With a human being, the inside grows old, full of regret, the mind senile. As the person decays inside, the wrinkles cut deeper."

The silent masses must have thought I was either incredibly mad or incredibly morbid.

Luckily, a student named Jason changed the subject around to Jimmy Nail's singing career.

As the conversation resumed its natural course towards pubs, clubs and *EastEnders*, I felt myself excluded once more, my pencil reluctantly returning to the lobster pots.

Simon knew about pubs and clubs from his uncle and cousin's conversation. However, his opinions on relationships could be bizarre.

When asked about women, he was indifferent. He had never mentioned being close to a woman in his life, save for in friendship.

"So, Simes, who do you fancy?" asked Rob, teasingly.

"Well I fancy that bonny Wayne, you, my bonny Rob, and bonny Uncle Derek, bonny Vince and good old bonny Damon!"

"What about girls? Any hot chicks on the scene?"

"Naaah! I love bonny men, I do!"

Laughter rose up as he giggled on bonny Rob's shoulder.

"Simon Hirst! You'll get talked about!"

Simon remained innocent. His idea of love may have appeared homosexual, but in reality it was more platonic. If he truly loved men, then he would have had good reasons to do so. He enjoyed rough and tumble with the lads, loved swapping yarns across the dinner table with his favourite male staff. They were close to him, and he was close to them. His friendships were always very loyal and emotional. He loved his friends.

His friendships expanded wider with the arrival of Lorraine, a new classroom worker. A happy-go-lucky eighteen-year-old blonde with wild hair, she always made time for Simon. Soon, he found himself missing her at the end of every shift.

"I love Lorraine!" he would cry with anguish.

In the past, he had written Peter Samson's name on his textbooks, but now he wrote hers.

Lorraine drove a bottle-green Chevette, an ancient relic given to her by her father as a present for passing her driving test. Not only did Simon love Lorraine, but he loved her car. When she later exchanged it for a Vauxhall Carlton, he vowed to buy the same car exactly down to its cherry red paint.

Deacon was growing more attached to Roisin. Together, they would discuss everything from motorcycle maintenance to Morrissey.

When the principal had told Deacon to remove his poster of *The Terminator* from his walls, Roisin had hidden it inside her locker before returning it to him on the principal's absence. Deacon, eternally grateful, had showered her with hugs and kisses. They would have done the Great North Run together, had it not been for an increase in Deacon's licking.

Meanwhile, I had my own interest in male staff. Kieran was still an old, untouchable flame, and even Vince and Damon were receiving admiration. When Marie, needing to settle with some rowdy young people at the kite festival, had left Damon and myself in charge of their son, Kris, I had admired the way father and son had played together amongst the flying sails.

Outside, in the normal world, I was still mortally afraid of men, even Gerald, for he had rejected my last three offers, so male staff provided comforting fantasies.

I had a lot of affection inside me, but not the correct means of how to express it.

– TWENTY-SEVEN –

I WAS SEVENTEEN, a virgin, and had never shared a proper relationship. Within the walls of Sternoake such unions with the opposite sex were still frowned upon as taboo, the irony being that many of the staff were in relationships themselves, most of them married. Perhaps the unit deemed people with autistic spectrum disorders unsuitable to form such bonds.

Many of the young people with more profound forms of autism were caught within the bubbles of their own tightly enclosed individual worlds. On the surface, it all seemed: "Me! Me! Me!" However, even the most reclusive or antisocial showed signs of affection. Sometimes it was cupboard love; often Gareth would hug Roisin in return for his twiddle; but sometimes that young person needed that closeness that can only be found in trusted company. Most of these relationships were grounded on extreme friendship. There was rarely any sexual intent.

Naive and unfamiliar with the usual aspects of sexuality, many young people were unaware of the uses of their genitalia. Deacon was slightly more aware, yet did not know the social rules that applied. On occasions, he would walk the corridor naked, unaware of the stir that it would cause. Elena would refer to her vagina and her periods with pet names learned from staff. Others would play with theirs, often receiving an unkind reaction. Their adolescence was spent in almost complete sexual innocence.

My own virginity annoyed me. Although I wished to be rid of it, to be normal, I would often freeze at the thought of intercourse. It would probably hurt and be embarrassing. I would be too reluctant to remove my clothes, or even submit to another person's desires. Like many people with Asperger's syndrome, I wanted a relationship, but also found myself struggling over how to accomplish one.

I could not form a relationship with a member of staff. That would be illegal. Refused by Gerald after a number of not-so-valiant attempts, I would find it too hard to form one with a "normal" person. In truth, I was trapped.

My only choice was escapism: the familiar return to the world of my beloved celebrities. I would fool myself that I actually stood a chance with one of the faces above my bed. Through years of experience, I could lucid dream. All I had to do was wake up for a few seconds, place the dream in my head, then fall back into slumber. I was less in control of the lucid dream than I was of my fantasies, but it was practice for real-life relationships. I had progressed to imagining real people as well as stars.

The World Cup arrived and hundreds of exotic, exciting and glamorous foreign footballers appeared on the screens. I found myself in daydreamer's heaven. As the Irish played, I would imagine myself in the green-shirted arms of Niall Quinn or Jason McAteer. As the Dutch played, I was in Ruud Gullit's embrace. As Gabriel Batistuta raced across the pitch for Argentina, I imagined him holding me tight under the searing sun.

I knew nothing of the inner workings of their souls, or their personalities off the pitch. I imagined them the way I wanted them to be. I gave them "real" personalities that were compatible with my own.

To one particular player I grew attached: attached near to the point of obsession. That player was Roberto Baggio. After he missed the penalty in the final, I felt for him. Branded a loser, he wept on the pitch, head hung low.

I naturally identified with losers. Being a loser at school, triumph was often snatched away from my grasp. This pessimistic attraction formed the strong bond between a young woman with Asperger's and a flickering figure on the T.V. screen. As he walked away, dejected, I imagined comforting him as our bond became more passionate.

At home, my sister once cut out a tiny picture of him from a newspaper to bribe me with. I was to sleep on the floor so her dubious friend could sleep in the bed. Normally, I would have said: "NO WAY!" When Roberto Baggio was involved, I agreed.

When I found out that he was married to a beautiful model, I cried. Obsessions not only brought me escapism: they also brought me commitment, possessiveness and moments of desperation, a bit like a real relationship.

"Roberto's leaving his wife!" I would tell the staff. "He's running away with me!"

"Where to?"

"To Sheffield," I would smile. "We're going to build a little castle there."

At night, all alone in my room, I would sit writing abominable poetry dedicated to Signor Baggio. Simultaneously, I would plan my escape from Sternoake, and his escape from his wife, who was, in my head, a beautiful battleaxe. All the men I idolised seemed to be married to models. This sent me into despair. Half-heartedly, I would fool myself that they would run away with me because I wrote them poetry, even if most of it was so bad it ended up as shreds in the bin.

One day, my head possessed me to start writing a short novel, which I hid inside my notebook. Illustrated with scrawls of ink, it was titled *One of the Lads*. The story involved a girl torn between an arrogant football captain and the team's passionate new Italian signing. I wrote letters to Italy, coining a few words from a phrase book, sending team portraits I had drawn. In return, I received a signed photograph. Although Baggio's autograph was duplicated, I was happy for weeks. My world had crossed over from fantasy to concrete fantasy.

My crazy, romantic notions never led me anywhere, save into the world of scrawls, doodles and illusions. When walking through the town, I would search the crowds, through the corner of my eye, for anyone who shared characteristics with my fantasy man. Rarely did I find a perfect clone. Reality did not have a factory in which to produce them.

– TWENTY-EIGHT –

WENDY HAD NO front teeth. She had removed them herself two years ago whilst within the confines of the quiet room. Nobody knew why she did it, even Wendy showed no regret at their loss. Through a Minnie the Minx smile, she whistled along to the radio.

Bert supervised the clippie mat. With a shining watch and rattling keys, he attracted Wendy's attention like a walrus-mustachioed diamond. As each rag was prodded into the design, her eyes and ears followed the jingle-jangle of his movements.

The clippie mat bored me. In fact it bored everyone save for Bert and his willing concubine. Hands on autopilot, my head imagined Gerald dancing away in some nightclub. Roisin had informed me that he was gay, but I had refused, point blank, to believe her. Perhaps he was bisexual – liked the tall blond he was often seen with, but liked girls also. That was possible. My heart then realised that it had gone off Gerald anyway, so it didn't really matter what his sexual orientation was.

"I like your watch, darling! Keysssss!" grinned Wendy through broken piano keys.

I, personally, thought it was an ugly, outdated watch, but Wendy had peculiar tastes.

"Pretty, pretty watch, darling!"

Wendy had recently been introduced to the "Leavers' Group", a breakfast club for the veteran residents of Sternoake. I was one of those veterans. Together, we sat at the Big Table, making our own toast and supervising our own cereal intake. Stationed in the domestic science room, we were each given numbers on our arrival for duties. I always insisted on number 9: *put the cereal on the table.* That gave me the advantage of getting to the Fruit n' Fibre first.

Sometimes Vince would liven up the proceedings by pretending that he was King Arthur and we were his Knights of the Big Table. Bob Ruxton was more difficult to get along with. If I dropped something, he would delight in scattering the cereal across the floor and watching me pick it up piece by piece. He called these games "Round-up!" and "Sheepdog!". I just called them "Bullshit".

Usually, there was guaranteed to be a fight in the Leavers' Group. Deacon would lick the floor and have his peanut butter confiscated by Bob. Simon, in despair at the injustice of it all, would try to escape to the dining room to sit with Uncle Derek. When caught, Simon would lose his cool, scattering boxes and breaking china like a hysterical torpedo.

I wasn't overly fond of the situation. I knew why we had been moved to the domestic science room, made to wash up after ourselves every morning instead of passing our bowls to the hatch in the dining room. Sternoake was housing too many residents and our placing and duties were the result of overcrowding.

After breakfast, assembly was particularly embarrassing. At the age of seventeen, I was still expected to sing *The Rainbow Song* with the others. Instead of singing "Red and yellow and pink and green…" like the rest of the congregation, I sang "Blue and white and blue and white…". Nobody noticed, but my quiet rebellion encompassed the colours of Sheffield Wednesday football club.

Assembly taught us the Green Cross Code and how to be polite. I suffered through it before setting off to college. I was glad my classmates could not see my humiliation each morning.

Despite these regular annoyances, I was beginning to see some of the staff as being people, friends. Some were still wardens of terror in my eyes, but there were others, like Damon and Vince, with whom I could have regular conversations. Sometimes, I wished I had met them in different circumstances. I wished I could have seen them from the start as human beings, rather than authority. Marie even defied authority herself at times.

Under the rule of Uncle Derek, my group, as usual, had been placed on the rota for flower pressing. Marie, who was leading the group, only had to see the ocean of bored faces around her to know that Derek's rule must be unwritten.

"Anybody fancy a kickabout?" she suggested.

It was muddy outside, the rain pouring down. Even Rhiona didn't seem keen.

"An *indoor* kickabout?"

Inside, I felt thrilled. At that moment, an indoor kickabout seemed the height of rebellion.

"Okay then! Right! Last one downstairs gets the duvet!"

Pelting downstairs, Marie led the troops to uncertain victory. Hollering to Simon at the back, she stormed into the corridor, face smiling wide as the doors flew open.

"I'll go in goal!" offered Simon, bouncing the ball off the wall.

"Let's shoot penalties!" suggested Marie. "You've got a hard job, Simon!"

Marie had played for a women's team as a teenager. Nicknamed "Lady Maradona" by her teammates, she was the natural candidate to be our captain.

"Goooooaaaaal!" she yelled as the ball flew past Simon.

Rhiona and I ran up to her in celebration, hugging her like a human duvet.

We split into two teams: three on each side. Simon, Marie and myself against Rhiona, Adam Greenman and Deacon.

"I'll be Gazza!" laughed Rhiona. "He's me favourite."

"Yer always cryin' like lallall Gazza," said Simon, resuming his position as goalie.

The ball flew to my feet. Running with it, uncertain at first, I picked up speed and went past Adam Greenman. Determined to get it past Deacon, I passed Rhiona. Before I could trip or stumble, I kicked the ball with all my might. It smashed past Deacon into the goal before bouncing up and hitting the overhead light. Looking up from the floor, I saw that the light had dislodged itself. Suddenly fear crept in.

THEY ALL WANT TO BE THE "CENTRE FORWARD" OF ATTENTION!

"Red card for that dirty player, Jessica Peers!" boomed Adam Greenman.

"Shit! I think I broke the light," I apologised.

"We'll sort it out," offered Simon. "We'll tell bonny Uncle Derek that lallall Peter Samson done it!"

"Peter Samson didn't do it," I panicked. "I did it, but I'll apologise."

We continued the game, but dread kept building in my heart. I was a rebel, yet I was an apologetic rebel. In the end I decided not to apologise and keep quiet about the whole thing. Together, Lady Maradona and I were quite a team. Adam Greenman ran out of puff easily, due to his membership of the Pompous Brothers' Smoking Club. Naturally, we exploited this.

A poster for road safety fell from the wall as I slid past Rhiona.

"I'm not Gazza now!" she grinned. "I'm playing for Brazeeel!"

The road safety poster was trampled beneath our feet.

This was not only an unusual football match, but an unusual event altogether. Normally there would have been a fight over who was going to be centre forward. Cries of "I want to be Alan Shearer!" were usually to be heard.

Usually, the game would consist of several goals and a goalkeeper gone A.W.O.L. One of the less able residents would usually be lumbered with this unfulfilling role, whilst those of us with Asperger's would try to hog the glory.

However, on this occasion we had worked as teams. The corridor was in pieces, but we had played together.

– TWENTY-NINE –

STANDING ON THE stairs of the ever-polished doorway of Sternoake, feeling the ground beneath my platformed shoes, I breathed in the cold air as it stung my nostrils. The rust of the hinges and the debris of visiting feet had been cleared safely away, leaving only a smooth, grey surface. Looking down at the relentlessly scrubbed stone, I knew that this would be the last time I would be standing here as a resident.

Still running through the palms of my hands, soon to turn cold from the numbing March air, was the heat of the common room radiator, by which I would usually stand, hand upon hip, the other hand armed with a felt-tip pen. I had left some doodles and caricatures as keepsakes. Some had been hung on the wall.

Around my shoulders, I could still feel the imprint of each embrace: some openly sincere, others restricted and dutiful. Some were well-meaning and dramatic.

Ideally, I would have stood for an immeasurable stretch of time, after weeping all my goodbyes into a trail of heartfelt tears, before slamming shut the exit of the doorway, suitcase placed strategically by my side, wandering slowly and heavily towards a single black taxi. On this occasion, I merely packed all my belongings into the boot of Dad's car, stopping at regular intervals to indulge in an extra hug and goodbye. Shaking beneath my clothes, I felt myself grow, at once, weak enough to feel my knees lose the will to support my heavy legs, and strong enough to lift the heavy cases that flocked by my feet. Dad helped me with my stereo, hauling it into the boot.

Genuine feelings, however, disappeared on the farewell appearance of Uncle Derek. Behind him stood a flock of residents, mainly echolalic and well-rehearsed, chanting "Goodbye! Goooodbye!" in unison. They had been forced to do it. Beneath those words that had been taught to them, the meaning was that of a bigger bedroom and the possibility of a newcomer to Sternoake coming to reside.

The gang had assembled, Simon, Rhiona, Elena, Deacon, Peter Samson, to wish me well. I promised that I would return to see them; after all, I knew I would be lonely in the future.

I wondered if Shaun had felt the same way on his departure.

Hugging Joan Hart, I remembered how we had shared a room together. She had loved my Oasis tapes. I had let her borrow them in return for being allowed to watch *Football Italia* on my portable T.V. late at night. Neither of us had complained to the other. We had become friends. I had got her out of trouble, she had been there as a good companion. We had played games and laughed together. I would miss that.

Although at times I had detested the place, opposed to its strict rota of activities, I would miss the company. Although I had constantly hated dinner times, being removed from the table for swearing or making gestures, I found that I would even miss being challenged by such rules. The rebel in me found constant pleasure through disobedience.

I was in the real world now.

The real world was unsanitised. The real world had no staff to watch out for mistakes. The real world had no programmes or free-time activities, no plans in black and white, no duvets, no chatter and songs in the domestic science room, no holding hands in a group on shopping trips, no jigsaw puzzles and battleships to keep people quiet, no going-to-bed times, no all-lads-in-the-bus-all-lasses-do-the-knitting, no time-schemes, no security checks, no rolling down the landing with Rhiona and Simon, no digging out the Big Book in remembrance of Shaun, no badly sung karaoke before supper at eight, no certainties. The real world had been compelling me to join it for so long, yet now it frightened me.

In the real world, there would be nobody to tell me what was "appropriate" or "inappropriate", nobody to correct my mistakes. I would have to make my own decisions after having them decided for me for so long. There would be nobody to tell me how to behave when in company, or advise me on the words that came from my mouth. Now it was all *my* responsibility. My actions now belonged to me. This, I was afraid of.

During the short period I had been given notice of my own departure, I had planned my exit in the style of Shaun Rogers. However, when the day came, I knew that to have played it funereal would have seemed, on my part, a macabre joke. In reality, both bitter and sincere, I would say my goodbyes without pretence. Like a character written out from the soap operas I so hated, I wished for my exit to remain open.

As I stepped into Dad's car, I felt a rush of tears well behind my eyes, yet I would cry in private. Some things were best left that way. The saline stung, anyway. My fear of germs was over. My fear of isolation was big.

For the first time in my life, I was genuinely *afraid*, not frightened, but *afraid*: about walking out into that big reality.

I knew that I would be living with Dad for a while. Dad was "cool", according to my friends. Dad was. Dad allowed me to socialise. He wanted me to have as near a normal social life as possible. I was still close to Dad, yet I knew that life would be so terrifyingly different.

One thing was certain, and that was the fact that I could not have stayed at Sternoake for ever.

As I took my steps towards the car, I looked over my shoulder to Simon's smile. Smiling back, holding in my thoughts, I gave a promise with my eyes.

I was eighteen.

As I waved from the passenger's window, I slipped my tape into the stereo. The music drowned out my memories. I knew that my mind could store friends and enemies like any of the best computers. They would always be there.

I could cope. I knew that I was in the running for two student awards, maths and English, from the college. That faded like daffodils left out in the sun.

Dad started the car. There was frost on the windows. As I borrowed his shades, I glanced back at the crowd. I would miss them.

The picture stayed in my head. The fights, the friends, the afternoons running through the ramshackle forest with Simon. It would never be forgotten.

Lightning Source UK Ltd.
Milton Keynes UK
05 November 2010

162417UK00001B/33/P